Straight from the Heart

Bonnie Tyler, born Gaynor Hopkins, was brought up in Skewen, a small village near Swansea. She grew up to become one of Wales' best-known performers, achieving chart success all over the world. She is recognised for her distinctive husky voice and a long list of hit singles including 'Total Eclipse of the Heart', 'It's a Heartache', 'Holding Out for a Hero', 'Lost in France', 'More Than a Lover', 'Bitterblue' and 'If I Sing You a Love Song'. In her fifty-year career, Bonnie has performed for audiences in countries across the world, and she has enjoyed critical acclaim for her recent albums *Rocks and Honey* and *Between the Earth and the Stars*. Her latest album, *The Best Is Yet to Come*, is a contemporary approach to the sounds and styles of eighties pop rock. Bonnie is currently working on new music and her 'Total Eclipse of the Heart' tour, marking forty years of her evergreen hit.

Straight from the Heart

BONNIE TYLER

CORONET

First published in Great Britain in 2023 by Coronet
An imprint of Hodder & Stoughton
An Hachette UK company

1

Copyright © Bandpick Limited 2023

The right of Bonnie Tyler to be identified as the Author of the Work has been asserted by her in accordance with the Copyright, Designs and Patents Act 1988.

A CIP catalogue record for this title is available from the British Library

Hardback ISBN 9781399726252
Trade Paperback ISBN 9781399726269
ebook ISBN 9781399726276

Typeset in Celeste by Hewer Text UK Ltd, Edinburgh
Printed and bound in Great Britain by Clays Ltd, Elcograf S.p.A.

Hodder & Stoughton policy is to use papers that are natural, renewable and recyclable products and made from wood grown in sustainable forests. The logging and manufacturing processes are expected to conform to the environmental regulations of the country of origin.

Hodder & Stoughton Ltd
Carmelite House
50 Victoria Embankment
London EC4Y 0DZ

www.hodder.co.uk

This book is dedicated to the precious loving memory of my wonderful parents, Elsie and Glyn Hopkins

Contents

Prologue

I followed a trail of M&M's to the door of a luxury apartment overlooking Central Park. As introductions go, it was an unusual one. But this was an unusual man.

He was the world-famous producer and songwriter Jim Steinman. And he was about to change my life.

CHAPTER ONE

Let the Show Begin

If you look back at my childhood, I would probably be the last person you would ever expect to be standing on a stage belting out rock anthems to crowds of tens of thousands of people.

I was brought up in a tiny village in Wales called Skewen, about seven miles outside of Swansea. Skewen is not picture-postcard perfect and not the kind of place where pop stars are crafted. There were no stage schools, no shops to buy fancy clothes, and the closest you could get to performing was singing hymns in the local church. So how on earth did I get from there to here?

To get to the 'here', we need to dive back into my early years. I was a very shy child, so I wouldn't have stood out in a crowd. My favourite things to do were hanging out at home with my (very big) family, seeing my friends or riding my bike and listening to music whenever I could.

I was always very content with my lot, and I never felt like I had anything to prove to the world. I was very at ease with being Gaynor Hopkins from Skewen. I had a lovely little life.

*

I think it was inevitable my parents were going to have a big family. My father was one of seven children, and my mother was one of nine. I grew up with three sisters and two brothers, and it was great having a big family. The house was always buzzing with people, and other relatives and friends were always popping in and out.

My gorgeous brother Paul is the youngest, and even though he's sixty now, he's still my baby brother. Next comes my beautiful younger sister Avis, who is four years younger than me. Then comes me (Gaynor), and then comes lovely Angela – or 'the diva', as her wife and friends call her – who is three and a half years older than me. Then we have our very handsome brother Lynn, who sadly passed away in his sleep when he was eighty. And finally, we have our fabulous sister Marlene, the eldest, who is eighty-three now but doesn't look it at all.

There aren't many photos of us when we were young, which is a shame. It's because my parents didn't always have a camera, but I was always saying to my mother, 'I must have been a bloody ugly baby, because I haven't seen one baby picture of me!' And she would say, 'Oh, don't be silly now . . . and stop swearing!' The first photo of me I can remember is one where I'm wearing a nurse's uniform, and I've got a dummy in my mouth and a doll under my arm. Angela is standing next to me, also in a nurse's uniform, and our mother is standing behind us.

I had a wonderful childhood. We lived in a four-bedroom council house in a cul-de-sac called Cwrt-Y-Clafdy. We were number 18, and we had a corner plot, which meant we had a big garden. My parents stored all sorts out there, and we could leave our bikes there unchained and know they wouldn't get stolen. It wasn't something we had to think about.

My parents always grew vegetables and loads of flowers. My father used to grow tomatoes, cucumbers and lettuces in his 'glasshouse'. There was hardly anything in the pantry most of the time, because it was all in the garden. It was like something out of *The Good Life*. There was still plenty of room for us kids to play, though.

We knew all the other people who lived on the road, and it was the kind of place where you never had to lock your door. Our door was always open, and anyone was welcome anytime. It was a proper community, which you don't get as often these days, sadly.

My grandmothers lived in the next cul-de-sac along, so they were always around, and I feel so grateful that I got to grow up always having them so close. My mother's mother – Mam Lewis, as I called her – had lots of chickens in her back garden. We used to love going over and feeding them.

We used to play cards with Mam Lewis regularly. She had a big wooden box of buttons, so we'd play for buttons instead of money. She had a green velvet tablecloth that she would lay out on her wooden living room table so it looked a bit fancier, and we would sit there for hours playing snap.

I loved that button box; I don't know where it went, but I wish I'd kept hold of it. Every one of those little buttons would probably hold a different memory for me now. I've got my own button box these days. I think it's one of those 'coming of age' things that happens to everyone somewhere along the line. I never understand where all the buttons come from, but I must have at least 200 going spare.

Mam Hopkins, who was my father's mother, was lovely

too. She had the most raucous laugh. She was the roly-poly, cuddly grandma. She was a pastry cook at the BP oil refinery near where we lived. She was so proud when the Queen Mother visited the refinery and said to her, 'Your pastry is some of the best I've ever tasted.' Oh, my grandmother was so chuffed with that, and we used to tell everyone that her pastry had the royal seal of approval! The Queen Mother wasn't wrong, either. Mam Hopkins's cooking and baking were so good I'm surprised we weren't all ten times the size. We all loved her spotted dick!

I was always told that Mam Hopkins had some kind of healing powers, although I know some people are very funny about that kind of thing. People often said that she was a natural healer and they were very drawn to her. I didn't experience it myself, but I know she was said to have helped a lot of people. I wish I'd learned more about it all from Mam Hopkins when she was still with us. I got to hear the stories from my mother, and I do think Mam Hopkins had something special about her.

We weren't ever left with babysitters, because we'd just go and see one of our grans if our parents had to go out somewhere together. As we got older, Marlene or Lynn would come over and look after us. We all had a really close bond, and I think growing up in a family like that sets you up for life. I came from a very secure background, and even though I was shy, I was always happy.

Because there was a twelve-year age gap between Marlene and me, she always seemed to be out of the house. But she was obviously working all the time, and then she was out in the evenings with her very handsome husband-to-be, Gwyn.

These days we're very close, and my husband Robert and I go on lots of holidays together with the two of them.

I'm also very close to my sister Angela. Angela was married with three children before she and her wife Jan got together – so was Jan. They had both married young and had their families. Later in their lives, one evening they were at the same party and just clicked. They started seeing each other, went on holiday and really enjoyed each other's company. So that's Angela and Jan's love story! Jan has made my sister so happy. Apart from her kids, she's the best thing that's ever happened to Angela.

*

We weren't what you'd call a well-off family, and we didn't have much money most of the time – or any of the time, really – but I didn't ever feel like I missed out on anything when my friends went on fancy holidays or got something new. I didn't mind hand-me-downs, because I knew my mother and father always did the best for us.

Sometimes, my mother would have to rent a washing machine and a clothes wringer to get all the laundry done. If she couldn't afford to, she would have to wash all the clothes in the bath and then hang everything outside or around the house to dry. Can you imagine doing that for all of us? It must have been never-ending. It wasn't the norm for every household to have washing machines like it is now, and my mother had to do it the hard way.

We had an outside toilet for years, and I used to be terrified of going out in the dark with all the spiders, so I would hold off going for as long as possible and then run out and back as fast as I could. Thankfully, by the time I was in my teens, the local council had built toilets inside our house, but it's amazing how quickly things have changed. No one would buy a house without an inside toilet these days unless they were going to renovate it!

Even though I had so many siblings, we all got on very well. Because there were so many of us, we had to share rooms. At one point, Avis, Angela and I slept in one bed together. We had a feather bed; at bedtime, my mother used to puff it up as much as she could, and us girls would run and jump on it before we settled down to go to sleep. Angela got married and left home at seventeen, so it was just Avis and I sharing a room then, and we loved spreading out on our comfy bed.

My absolute pride and joy was my bike. I cycled everywhere as a kid, and that was when I felt most at peace. I got my first bike when I was nine, and my father taught me how to ride it. When he let me go, and I realised I was cycling on my own, I thought, 'Wow, I'm *doing* it!' It felt like I was going to take off! It was the same feeling you get when you pass your driving test. You feel like you've got so much freedom.

Loads of other kids lived around us, so we were always playing games outside on the road: games that kids probably wouldn't even have heard of these days, like hopscotch and mob. On other days, we would get together and go picking wild daffodils and blackberries, pushing along half a dozen prams with our dolls in them, or we'd cycle for miles, or go off to climb rocks.

I learned to be happy without having a lot, and to make something out of nothing. I'd look out of my window to my street, and I wouldn't see grey tarmac and houses bunched up close together – I'd see a playground, full of fun and possibility. Kids of all ages coming together to make the best of the summer days. All we needed was a ball and a rounders bat, and we could be out there for hours.

If you'd said to me back then that in fifty years, we would be able to talk to each other via watches, I would have thought you'd gone totally mad. It was such a fabulous time to grow up. We didn't have all the TV stations and gadgets, and I think having to make your own entertainment was a big part of why we were so happy. I'm glad I didn't live in a time when we had iPads, mobile phones and TVs in every room. They were simpler times when you appreciated the small things; there was never any sense that you had to have the latest trainers or the newest gadget. To me, having a bike and being able to go out and ride it whenever I liked was a dream come true – and then there was music, of course. Music and my bike were my life when I was a teenager. They were all I needed.

I know I am very lucky to have the nice things I have now, but I would be just as happy without them. I've learned time and time again that 'things' don't make you happy. People do. I have a lot more material possessions because everyone accumulates more as they grow up, but if you took it all away tomorrow, I'd still be a grateful person. I think that's because I didn't have much as a youngster, but I was still satisfied with my lot.

*

Aside from picking blackberries, my earliest memory is quite a sad one. I was about three years old, but I remember it so clearly. My father wasn't very well, which meant I had to start school early, so at three years old, I started nursery. My mother took me in for my first day, and I even remember what I was wearing – a little green plaid mac. When she let go of my hand for me to go into the nursery, I started crying my eyes out. My mother was trying really hard not to cry too.

I couldn't bear to leave her. The teachers could see we were upset, so one of them came over and told my mother that I would be alright. She took me by the hand and walked me in with her.

The funny thing is, I don't remember a huge amount about my childhood after that, but I can picture every detail of that day like it was yesterday. Maybe because it was traumatic for me?

I was born on 8 June 1951. Everyone was still suffering from the fallout of the war, but we younger kids were sheltered from it. I feel incredibly lucky that I was born after it had taken place. We knew what had happened, and we knew our father was suffering as a result of what he'd seen during his time as a soldier, but I think when you're young, you can't get to grips with what a massive, life-changing event it was. It was only when I got older I was able to understand it better.

My father was classed as disabled because he had tuberculosis. I think he also had PTSD from the war, although you didn't call it that in those days. I don't think there was even a term for it. He was on the beach at Dunkirk, and he saw some horrific things. His brother-in-law, Uncle Frank, was stationed alongside him, and my father saw him shot dead in front of his eyes. He didn't want to leave Frank in the middle of a field, so he dragged him back to the British camp, but of course, there was nothing they could do for him. It must have been unbearable to experience something so traumatising. How can you ever get over something like that?

Quite often, after a few drinks, my father would talk about Uncle Frank and get very upset. So, while he wasn't wounded physically in the war, it had undeniably affected him – probably more than we know. It was normal to see soldiers who had injuries from the war – both mental and physical – so that didn't ever shock me. But when my father would tell us stories of what it was like, it was hard to comprehend. So many people had been through so much, and you didn't have the amazing mental health services you get these days. Despite my father's trauma, he put on a brave face in front of us young ones. He used to tell us some really funny stories that happened to him when he was a kid too, and some of the songs he used to sing to us were very, *very* naughty. We used to laugh our heads off!

Years later, my sister Marlene and her husband Gwyn took my father on the Eurostar to Dunkirk in France to visit the church and the memorial to all the lost soldiers. He wanted to pay his respects to Frank, but it was difficult for him. Every time I think about the war and how senseless it was, it breaks my heart. All those loved ones taken, and for what? It was hard on so many people, and I don't think it's something you can ever really leave behind.

Our house was always a happy one, but the threat of another war loomed over us like a black cloud. For years after the Second World War ended, there was talk of another one coming, and it haunted my mother. She was terrified that my brother Lynn would be called up, and it really played on her mind, which I can understand. It was a terrible worry for both my parents, not least because there was talk of nuclear bombs and all sorts. Thankfully, it didn't come to anything, but I think because they had both lived through the utter horror of the Second World War, there was always this fear that something else could happen.

I imagine that when you have experienced something like that, the fear of something similar taking place never really leaves you, especially when you've got children who would be expected to do their bit for the country. I think a lot of parents felt the same around that time.

*

As time went on, my father's tuberculosis got better, and he got a lot stronger. The spark came back into his eyes. I remember him always being quite fit; he used to walk everywhere, and in his teens, he used to earn a bit of money to give to his mother by taking part in boxing matches. You would never have known it to look at him, though. He was a beautiful-looking man. Almost angelic, with the bluest eyes – I'm lucky to have inherited my father's blue eyes.

Once he was better, my father was able to return to work. He'd worked as a coal miner before I was born, but he only did that very briefly when he was a young man. Then he went to work at the Country Maid Bakery, but the doctor told him he had to stop working there because the flour was affecting him, and to go back on streptomycin to treat his tuberculosis.

My mother didn't ever work because she had so many of us to look after. It was very hard for her because she had to do all the washing and cooking and cleaning. You rarely saw her sitting down taking a breather. She always put us first. On Sundays, we'd go blackberry picking, and she would make tarts and cakes for us all to eat during the week. The house always smelled incredible when we got back from chapel. Like the best cake shop you can imagine. I loved walking into the house and being hit by a wave of sugar and sponge.

When I was seven, she took me to see a musical that was put on at All Saints Church in Skewen. It was the first time I'd ever heard the song 'There's No Business Like Showbusiness' by Irving Berlin, and I loved it. I think that's where I first got the bug for performing. I wouldn't say boo to a goose, and yet there was a part of me that yearned to sing in front of people.

When I was about ten, I remember going singing and marching through our village with the chapel, along with many of the other children who attended church. I felt very grand being a part of that, but the first time I ever sang on my own in front of other people was when I was about thirteen. I sang 'All Things Bright and Beautiful' during a church service one Sunday, and I felt a real buzz afterwards.

Quite often on a Sunday, us kids used to go to chapel in the morning and afternoon, and then in the evening, we'd go to church. I think it was a good way for my mother to get us all out of the house so she and my father could have some peace and quiet – and some time on their own, if you know what I mean.

My parents weren't Bible-bashers, but all of my family have a strong belief in God and a strong faith. I think that's helped us through many hard times. I stopped going to church a lot when I was around seventeen, but I think it was good for me growing up. It teaches you right from wrong and how to be a good person. I don't think it does anybody any harm, and I took countless positive things away from going for all those years.

*

Music was a huge thing in our house. A record player brought us more joy than anything else, and people used to stand outside listening to my mother singing because she had such an incredible voice. She would be doing the housework with the windows open, and people would stop by our hedge because her voice was so beautiful. She would sing everything from opera to 'Itsy Bitsy Teenie Weenie Yellow Polka Dot Bikini'. There was none of this 'Shhh, the baby's sleeping' or neighbours getting cross; they all enjoyed it. It was always music, music, music, all the time, from the moment you woke up until you went to bed, so I think it was inevitable that some of us became singers.

We had a piano in the house. I can't play, but everybody used to have a tinker and try and play it by ear while other people sang or danced. My mother had a radiogram and a big pile of 78s, and then when 45s came out in the sixties, my siblings started buying those, so we would play them at home. I used to get *so* excited when one of them came home with a new song.

My brother Lynn was into Eddie Cochran and rock 'n' roll. We'd roll up the carpet in the living room, push the furniture up against the walls and jive. My cousin Dorothy and my next-door neighbour Anne would come over. They were both really good jivers, and we'd all dance to all these wonderful records. Elvis's 'You Ain't Nothin' But a Hound Dog' was a big favourite. Lynn bought some Brylcream so he could fashion his hair into a quiff like Elvis, and he bought some crepe-soled shoes and a long jacket to get the full look. My mother was absolutely horrified when she saw him decked out in all that gear. She ended up giving the clothes away when someone knocked on the door asking if we had anything we could donate to those in need. Lynn was gutted. He loved those shoes and that jacket. Goodness knows what whoever got his hand-me-downs must have thought.

Marlene loved Perry Como and Frank Sinatra, and my mother always used to play Mario Lanza and opera. It was very eclectic music-wise in our house. I grew up surrounded by a lot of different sounds and styles, and it was all fascinating to me.

I was in love with the Beatles, but I didn't often get a chance to play my records because my older siblings had their friends round to dance, and no one was quite as passionate about the Beatles as I was at the time. Angela understood, though, and gave me my first album: *A Hard Day's Night*. I soon knew that album word for word. I played it over and over, to the point where I'm surprised I didn't wear it out. Even now, if I hear one of the songs from that album, I'm transported back to that time, and I can feel the same love I had for it back then.

The very first record I bought myself was *Hippy Hippy Shake* by the Swinging Blue Jeans. I was thirteen, and I played that record to death. I'm surprised it lasted so long.

I remember watching the girls on *Top of the Pops* and thinking, 'I could do that!' There was a *ting*. A spark. A small bit of me thought . . . *Maybe. Maybe there is a way to get there*. But I didn't know how to begin trying – the lives of the people I saw on *Top of the Pops* seemed so different to mine, as if they'd been *born* to be famous. And here was me, living in a tiny village in Wales, with no contacts and no way of getting noticed. I passed it off as a silly dream and resigned myself to a life that was going to be happy and homely.

I used to sing in my bedroom a lot, but I didn't have a microphone or a karaoke machine like all the kids have now. Oh, I would have loved that, but there was no such thing back then. What we did have was a reel-to-reel two-track tape recorder. My father bought the machine because my mother's sister, my Auntie Audrey, had emigrated to Canada with her husband, David. We used it to make tapes so that we could send them to her, and she could send tapes back to us to let us know what she'd been up to. That tape recorder would be considered an antique these days, but I thought it was very cutting-edge at the time. When Daddy came up with the idea of recording *Top of the Pops* on it, it was like all my Christmases had come at once.

Every time he recorded an episode, I'd take the recorder up to my bedroom with a writing pad and a pen, and I would go through the whole tape and make a note of the songs I loved. Then I'd listen back and keep pressing pause until I got all the words written down. I used to sing them into my hairbrush for hours and hours, and that's how it all started for me. I fell in love with singing just from doing that. Looking back, even then my voice had a husky tone to it, but I didn't think much of it. I thought everyone's voices were different from each other's.

My favourite songs to sing were 'Anyone Who Had a Heart' by Cilla Black, 'Piece of My Heart' by Janis Joplin and anything by Nina Simone, Tina Turner, Wilson Pickett or Otis Redding. I loved soulful music, and I think the sixties and seventies had some of the best music that's ever been made.

Tina Turner and Janis Joplin were probably the ones that stood out most to me back then. I'd sing into the mirror, dreaming of being like them. I didn't know much about Janis when I was a naive teenager. I didn't even really know what she looked like, because teen magazines weren't yet a big thing, so for me, it was all about how she sounded. Her voice enchanted me. I'd sing 'Cry Baby' at the top of my voice. I heard someone who put her heart completely into her songs and was so gifted.

It was only when I got older and read about her that I realised how tragic her life had been and came to understand how tormented she was. She hated the way she looked and felt ashamed of herself. As a result, she tortured herself by doing everything that was bad for her, and you can hear the pain in her songs. Everything comes from the heart. It's not pitch-perfect, but it's raw, and it's real. Drink and drugs seemed to be her main problem, and it's heartbreaking to think that she couldn't see what others saw, which is how talented and brilliant she was.

When I discovered radio in my early teens, it was so liberating to hear all this pop music for free! I used to tune in to Radio Luxembourg, and I still remember now that it was 208 medium wave. I'd listen to it at night, and it played a huge part in shaping me. It was transmitted from Luxembourg because the BBC held the exclusive licence to all radio stations in the UK, which meant no one could simply set up a radio station and start broadcasting. The station's way of getting around it was to broadcast from abroad. It was horribly crackly sometimes, but I didn't care. I was just so thrilled that I could listen to music whenever I wanted to.

Radio 1 started in September 1967, and the DJ I always loved was Tony Blackburn. I still think he's brilliant with his silly jokes. He used to play a lot of Tamla Motown and R&B. Imagine going from having to buy records to be able to hear your favourite artists to turning on a box in your room and hearing them coming out of there instead. It was like magic!

I used to love listening to the *Billy Cotton Band Show* on a Sunday. He would have different artists on there, and I still remember Carole King singing 'Will You Love Me Tomorrow?', and one of my early favourites, 'It Might as Well Rain Until September'. She had a beautiful voice.

When radios got smaller, we would take them down to the beach with us and dance on the sand in the warm sun. It was amazing. Such simple, small things made me feel so good.

*

It was a good job my home life was so lovely, because school was a nightmare. It was never a happy time for me. They say your schooldays are the best days of your life, but mine certainly weren't. I was downright miserable. Back then, we all had to pass our eleven-plus to go to grammar school. Lots of girls in my class did, but I didn't – probably because I didn't take it!

The day I was supposed to do mine, I told my mother I was ill with a stomach ache because I couldn't face doing it. What she didn't know was that I could have rearranged it and done it another time, but I kept quiet about that.

I was being bullied a bit at the time, and I didn't want to end up at the same school as the bullies again, so I decided if I failed, at least they wouldn't be able to make my life a misery anymore. My plan was to go to the same comprehensive school as my sister Angela, so she could keep an eye out for me and protect me if I needed her to. I was only a little thing, petite and quite introverted, so I was an easy target.

I got bullied because I sometimes got Angela's hand-me-downs, while most of the other girls would come back after the summer holidays with posh new outfits. But if you weren't very well-off, hand-me-downs were what you wore in those days. I didn't see anything wrong with it.

There was one girl who was head of a gang, and she was really mean. She'd gather everyone around her and then say, 'Who's the prettiest girl in school?' and we'd all have to say, '*You are.*' She used to come to school really dressed up, and obviously had a wealthier family. I felt like she looked down on me.

I got my own back on her eventually. We all started going to the Top Rank club in Swansea when we were in our late teens. One night, she came in with this guy called Phil, who was very good-looking. I'd taken a shine to him. He had a white Triumph car with a black soft top, which was very cool in those days. She still thought she could bully; she came over and said, 'Gaynor, give me my sixpence so I can put my coat in the cloakroom.'

I was older and much stronger in myself by this point, so I told her to bugger off! I thought, *We're not at school now, you know.*

17

Guess who got a lift home with Phil that night?

Moi.

And then we started going out. She must have been fuming, but it made up for all those years she was so horrible to me. Phil moved to Australia, and funnily enough, years later, he came to see one of my shows with his wife, and we met up backstage. Another ex-boyfriend of mine, John, and his wife also came to see me perform in Australia. It's such a small world.

I have a habit of bumping into boys from my past, actually. My first-ever kiss was a little peck with a boy called Brian. I can't remember where we were at the time, but it was probably after finishing school. After I got married, I had roller blinds put in at my house, and guess who turned up to fit them?

I couldn't stand school. I would go as far as to say I hated it. All I wanted to do was sing; I've never been academic. Even though I was shy, I was also a bit of a joker because I found it quite hard to concentrate on subjects I didn't enjoy. I think people have different skills, and biology and physics were not among mine – though strangely, I was good at maths. I didn't enjoy sport at all. It was *not* for me. We used to have to run around the sports field in blue knickers in all weathers. When we got a bit older, we were given a choice of doing dancing lessons or sports, and although I'm not the greatest dancer, I started dance classes just to avoid going out in the rain.

It was clear I was never going to become a rocket scientist, but there were two teachers, both called Mr Davis, who really supported me. I always used to come last in history and Welsh, and at one point, both of them sat me down for a chat and encouraged me to concentrate and listen more, and not get so distracted in class. They must have spoken beforehand because they both said pretty much the same thing. They said they knew I could do better. The truth was, I wasn't being rubbish on purpose; I just wasn't very interested in the subjects. I found them boring, to be honest. My parents didn't speak Welsh at home, so it wasn't as if I was around it often and could pick it up. People tend to speak Welsh more in North Wales than in South Wales. But those talks must have helped because, by the time the exams came around, I came second in Welsh and fourth in history (out of about thirty-five students in my class). It shows that it does make a difference when you have good teachers supporting you and telling you to knuckle down.

I think part of my problem was that I'd had to take quite a lot of time off school when I was around twelve. Everyone in my year had the vaccine for tuberculosis. If the point where they injected you on your arm formed a bubble, it meant you might have tuberculosis, so you got sent home from school in case it was catching. My arm bubbled up, and because my father had been ill with it in the past, I think they were being very cautious.

I didn't ever have any symptoms or feel ill at all, but I had to stay home from school for eight or nine months. I remember the school sending me a big basket of fruit to make me feel better, but secretly I liked not being at school. I used to have to go to this clinic in the next village along, Neath, and have X-rays on my chest. They could see that I had scarring on both of my lungs, which meant I had suffered from tuberculosis at some point, but it had healed on its own.

The doctors couldn't understand it at all, and they kept saying it was miraculous. My mother always put it down to me riding my bike everywhere and taking in all the lovely fresh air. Goodness knows how I became a singer when both of my lungs were scarred. I've read a story about how a similar thing happened to Tom Jones, though, and we're both still going strong!

Once I was finally allowed to go back to school, all my friends and I started going down to The Ritz nightclub on Saturday afternoons, because they hosted a roller disco. It was such great fun going round and round, singing along to chart hits.

I also used to go to a youth club that was held in the old girls' school in Skewen. This lad used to play acoustic guitar, and I loved singing with him. There was a song at the time called 'Out of Time' by Chris Farlowe, and I absolutely loved it, so we sang that a lot and people would gather around to hear us.

I would walk back from youth club with my friend who used to live near me. In the autumn and winter, it was pitch black, and once she'd gone into her house, I used to run up the middle of the hill on my own and into our cul-de-sac like a bat out of hell because I was so terrified of the dark.

*

I left Rhydhir Comprehensive School as soon as I could, aged sixteen. I knew I wasn't going to go on to higher education once I left school. I wanted to get a job so I could buy make-up and clothes and go out dancing with my friends down at the Top Rank.

I left school for good on a Friday, and I was determined I was going to get a job and start work the following Monday. I didn't have any real qualifications, but on that Friday afternoon, I went around all the shops in Skewen. There was a main road that was a couple of miles long, and there were shops on both sides of it. I started right at the bottom, and I worked my way up one side of the street, calling in every single shop, asking if they had a vacancy for an assistant. Then I went across the other side of the road and did the same. By the end of the day, I had two jobs to choose from; one in a grocery shop and one in a collector's shop. In the end, I chose the grocery shop, and I started the following Monday, just as I promised myself I would.

I was earning peanuts, and I later discovered I was being paid below the minimum wage. In those days, an official used to go around all the shops and make sure people were being paid properly. They were very strict, and when this official realised I'd been underpaid for so long, my boss got a telling-off and a warning. My boss told me, 'I can make it up to you by giving you the extra money weekly in your wages, or I can just give you £100.' Well, I took the £100. Who wouldn't? I'd never had that much money in my life!

The first thing I did was buy myself some make-up, because I loved the look that was around back at the time. During my childhood, we used to go to a place called Happy Valley in Porthcawl every year and stay in a caravan for two weeks during the summer holidays. It was fantastic. We'd be down on the beach every day and at the fair every night. It was a child's dream. There was a dance hall in the grounds, but I wasn't old enough to go in. I always used to see a very glamorous girl with big black hair and false eyelashes who was often hanging around the doorway. She really stood out from the crowd, and I used to think, 'I'd love to wear make-up like that.' She looked like a proper sixties It girl, with a headband like the one Priscilla Presley wore and winged eyeliner. I was only young at the time, but I wanted to look that cool. I didn't have a headband or any make-up, but I decided I could make myself my very first pair of eyelashes. I must have been about thirteen, and I cut a bit of my hair off, and I got two strips of Sellotape and stuck these tiny little pieces of hair on to them, one by one. Then I rolled the Sellotape strips around a pencil to make them curly, and then I stuck them on. Of course, I thought I looked amazing. My mother asked me to pop next door and borrow something from our neighbour, Mrs Nicholas, and she looked at me as if I was completely ridiculous. And I can't deny it; I *did* look completely ridiculous. I had to make do with my home-made lashes, but the image of that girl stayed with me. So now, with my first job, as soon as I could afford to buy false eyelashes, I stocked up – and to this day, I couldn't be without them. Eyelure has made a fortune out of me over the years.

I paired my new eyelashes with Miners pale pink lipstick. Then I went straight to Woolworths to buy some records. I bought a Nina Simone album, because her vocals were so incredible, a Tina Turner album, and one called *Don't Break My Pretty Balloon,* by a lady called Vikki Carr. I used to play those albums on repeat and gaze at the covers. I always felt like I could see something new in the cover while I listened to the songs. I learned every song that way. I cherished all my albums, and they all helped to teach me to sing in some way. Believe it or not, I still own some of them to this day.

When I was working in the grocery, a lady called Mrs George was a regular, and I got to know her quite well. She cleaned at The Ritz nightclub and music venue, which got all the big names. Everyone from the Kinks to Long John Baldry played there.

I felt a bit brave one day, and I said to her that I would love to see one of the live bands. She agreed to sneak me in, and I watched mesmerised as a band I'd never heard of owned the stage. I felt almost breathless seeing people singing songs *right in front of me.* I was in complete awe. They weren't a band I'd ever heard of; they weren't famous or anything, but I was so impressed with them anyway.

When the band finished, I saw the female lead singer leave the stage and go to the bar to get a drink. I took a deep breath and walked over to talk to her. I was so nervous, but I told her how great I thought her band were, and then I said, 'Would you mind telling me, please, how did you get to be a singer in the band? I would love to do the same thing one day.'

She pushed past me like she was some kind of superstar and said, 'Excuse me, I'm going to the toilet.'

I'm not the kind of person who would ever do that to someone, but the way she treated me made me determined that if I ever made it, I would be nice and kind to anyone who ever wanted help or advice. It was like something inside me switched at that moment, and I thought, *Just you wait and see what I can do!* To this day, I stand by that rule. It takes the same amount of effort to be nice to someone as it does to be rude, so why not choose the more positive option? Being rude just doesn't make any sense to me.

I started going out to pubs around this time (they were a bit more relaxed with the underage rules in the sixties!). I had a friend who used to take a glass home with her every night. I have no idea why, but she would always sneak one home in her handbag for a bit of a laugh. I was out with her one night, and I'd had a glass of cider, so I decided to do the same. My mother found the glass in my bag the following day, and she made me take it back to the pub and tell them I was sorry. It was so embarrassing. She was such a gentle woman, but she didn't let us get away with anything. My friend, meanwhile, had this huge collection of them – her father even made a shelf to display hers, whereas I did it once and had to go back with my head hanging in shame. I never did do it again.

*

As I've mentioned, I come from a very large family, and my mother's sister-in-law Auntie Blodwyn (you don't get much more Welsh than that!), used to come and visit us all the time. She overheard me singing along to music in my room, and she said to my mother, 'Gaynor's always up there singing, and she's got a great voice. She ought to go in for a talent competition. There's one in the local rugby club in a couple of weeks. I'm going to put her name down for it.'

When she told me what she was planning to do, I said, 'Oh, no, please don't do that, please don't do that!' Working in a shop and meeting new people all the time hadn't made me any less shy. But strangely, despite my protests, a very, very small part of me wanted her to do it. I couldn't understand why, because it sounded petrifying, but a little voice deep down inside of me was saying, *What's the worst that can happen?*

In the end, after much pressing from Auntie Blodwyn, I agreed to let her put my name down. I didn't have any sheet music or anything, so I had to go to the local music shop to choose some songs. I decided I would sing 'Those Were the Days', a song by a fellow Welsh singer called Mary Hopkin that was number one in the charts at the time, and 'Will You Love Me Tomorrow?' by a very cool group called The Shirelles. I can't read music, but I bought the sheet music for those two songs at a music shop in Neath, so the organist and drummer could play them. Then my mother took me shopping and bought me a cream and gold Lurex dress to wear. It was the most fashionable thing I'd ever owned.

And so, in April 1969, a panicked seventeen-year-old made her way to her local rugby club wearing a gorgeous dress and a look of sheer terror. I'd never sung into a real microphone in my life, and I was scared my voice would come booming out and make the audience jump five feet in the air. As it turned out, people really enjoyed my performance. And, much to my surprise, so did I.

The first prize was £5, which would have bought me a lot of false eyelashes. In the end, I came second – to an accordionist, of all things – and won £1, which was still quite a lot of money back then. (That reminds me of one of my favourite childhood jokes: What's the difference between an accordion player and an onion? Nobody cries when you chop up an accordion.)

There were a couple of local agents at the show who booked

singers and acts for cabaret shows. They wanted to put me on their books, which was incredibly flattering, but I said to them, 'I haven't got any kind of repertoire. You've just heard my entire repertoire! I work in a shop usually, so I'm not a seasoned singer or anything. I just entered for a bit of fun.'

As I walked away, I thought, 'Have I just argued my way out of some professional singing work?'

Bert, the guy who owned the music shop where I bought my sheet music, also worked as an agent and said he wanted to put me on his books. He said he could get me some gigs, but again, I told him that the only songs I knew were the songs I sang in my bedroom, so I said no. It didn't feel like the right thing for me.

A few weeks later, there happened to be an advert in the *Swansea Evening Post* looking for three girls to join a harmony group. The group was going to be called Bobby Wayne and the Dixies. It said that no experience was needed and training would be given. Well, it could have been written for me!

Bobby Wayne was already singing in the Townsman Club in Swansea, which was a mixture of cabaret, dining and dancing. A guy called Ronnie Williams used to manage the music side of things and play the organ for the artists. I wrote this grovelling letter to Ronnie telling him that I thought I would be perfect for the group. I don't know where I got the courage to do that, but something about it felt right.

*

I was still working in the shop, but I was ready to move on. I didn't want to end up selling cabbages for the rest of my life, so I decided to start preparing myself just in case I got an audition. I worked all day, and then in the evening I would go down to my cousin Christine's house with a carrier bag full of records and we'd play them and sing along. Christine and I had grown up together, and we'd always shared a lot of music; I was always cycling to and from her house, laden down with my latest buys. We especially loved Thursdays because we could watch *Top of the Pops* on television, then listen to records in Christine's bedroom and imagine being on the stage singing.

Christine's mother, my Auntie Kate, was a wonderful woman, but she had it hard. She also had a proper temper on her. Sometimes when I went around, she'd be bawling and shouting at my Uncle Evan. If he ignored her, she'd open all the windows and bellow, 'Can you hear me now?' The whole street could hear her!

She was always behind on the rent, and sometimes we'd have to hide behind the couch when the rent man came around. One time, we were all there, crouched down behind the sofa in the back room, and I looked up to see the bloody rent man looking down at us! He had gone around the back of the house looking for Auntie Kate, and he had completely busted us. I didn't know whether to laugh or cry.

Auntie Kate was such a funny character, but you knew not to cross her. One of the things I loved about her was that she had really small feet, a size three, but she always wore six-inch stilettos. She had a big box of them (no wonder she couldn't pay the rent), and Christine and I loved tottering around in her heels when we were little, thinking we were all grown up.

I don't know how Auntie Kate wore them day in, day out.

She even used to do the shopping and housework in them. Maybe I take after her, because I love heels. I wonder if walking around the house for all those years in my auntie's stilettos prepared me for later life, because I used to play full concerts in high heels and not even think about it (though my heels are a bit lower these days!).

*

One evening, when I was walking down Burrows Road on the way to Christine's, this fancy blue Mercedes car pulled up next to me. I jumped away, wondering what the hell they were doing. I may have been a working woman by then, but I still listened to my mother when she told me not to speak to strangers.

I stood there, clutching my carrier bag of albums, and a gentleman leaned over and wound down the window on the passenger side of the car to reveal a very attractive lady with a poodle on her lap.

The man asked me if I was Gaynor Hopkins, and I was a bit taken aback.

'Yes, who wants to know?' I said.

He replied, 'I'm Ron Williams from the Townsman; you wrote me a letter. I've just been to your house, and your mother told us where you would be. Can you come to an audition at eleven-thirty tomorrow morning in Swansea?'

Tomorrow would be a Saturday, and I wasn't working, so of course, I said yes. When I got to Christine's house, I asked her if she would go with me to the audition. I knew I would be too nervous to go alone, and she was the perfect person to accompany me. We could even do a bit of practising on the way!

We travelled to the audition by bus the following morning, and I was so excited. The auditions were held in the Townsman Club, which was a huge venue with two floors. There were about thirty-five girls there in total, and we were all sitting in alcoves, waiting for our turn to sing for Ronnie.

When it was my turn, I sang 'Those Were the Days' by Mary Hopkin again, because I knew it like the back of my hand by then. I didn't think I had a chance of getting picked over all these gorgeous, talented girls, but – and I think you'll know the punchline to this one – I only went and got offered a slot as a Dixie!

Bobby Wayne had the most incredible high-pitched voice that reminded me of Frankie Valli from The Four Seasons. It was pitch-perfect and so beautiful, and I couldn't wait to be a part of his stage show. I felt like I'd *made* it!

I started working as a Dixie the same week, in May 1969, just a month after I'd entered the talent competition. We all had to have stage names, and one of my nieces was called Shereen, so I named myself after her and then added the surname Davis. I've had a few different names in my time, haven't I?

I was so nervous on my first night. My only other experience of singing in front of people that weren't friends and family had been at the talent competition, and that had been a small event. Now, all of a sudden, I was gearing up to sing in front of a seasoned crowd of club regulars who were expecting a polished, professional performance. I wasn't sure I could offer either of those things.

At least I'd had some of my family at the talent show support-ing me. Here, I was totally on my own, aside from my fellow

Dixies, Sue Lambert and Toni Carol. We had been taught where to stand, how we should dance and all the other basic instructions, but I could feel all that essential information making its way out of my brain the closer to walking out on stage we got.

The other two Dixies and I shared a dressing room at the side of the stage. For our debut performance, we all dressed up in matching outfits and then waited for Bobby to invite us on to the stage.

'Ladies and gentlemen, I give you the Dixies!' I heard Bobby boom into the microphone.

My head started swimming with all the things that could go wrong, and my legs began to tremble, but I knew I had the girls by my side. We walked on to blinding light and an appreciative crowd and took our places behind Bobby. It seemed to take forever for Bobby to start singing a song (please don't ask me what it was – I think my anxiety-ridden brain has blocked it out), but as soon as we started to sing, my nerves seemed to fade away, and I began to enjoy myself. I couldn't believe it! We Dixies felt very natural together, and when we walked off the stage, I felt a high I can't explain. Not like a drug high (not that I'd know, mind) but a mixture of pride and relief. I'd bloody done it!

When I first started singing in the nightclub, my father wasn't very happy about it at all. Clubs had a bit of a reputation as places where flash wide boys hung out, and he was worried about me being so young. Also, his friends down the pub used to say to him, 'We hear your daughter's working in the Townsman Club. How do you feel about that?' I think he got a bit sick of that too. But after a while he warmed to the idea, and he and my mother used to come dancing with my

Auntie Kate and Uncle Evan, and they had a fabulous time. They used to love it.

At first, I was only working two nights a week, while still working at the grocery. We started at 8pm and did three forty-five-minute stints during the evening. We had to learn loads of songs and how to harmonise with each other, as well as take turns to do lead vocals.

It was great training because we were singing all styles of music. In those days, people used to come to the Townsman Club to dance to the bands. This was years before DJs started going around all the clubs playing songs. It was proper live music with a real mixture of sounds, so there was something for everyone. There was a lot of work for resident singers in the sixties and seventies. Every club or hotel had either a jazz band or some sort of four-piece vocal band, and they always needed female and male singers to do backing vocals. That suited me. I wasn't sure if I'd ever be the sort of singer who could take centre stage. I was nervous enough singing alongside other people. I hated having to talk in between songs so much that I ended up having some elocution lessons so I would sound a bit more elegant. I went to this lady called Miss Davina Powell for quite a while. While I was with her I would sound quite posh, but the minute I left I was back talking like I always had. I still have this thick, broad Welsh accent, and I have never lost it.

I bump into my teacher every now and again back home, and she says she follows my career and she's pleased I kept my accent. I'm pleased too. It's who I am, and I'm glad I didn't change it after all.

*

The only pain was getting to and from work every night. I couldn't always get a lift, and the bus took forever, so I'd have to get up for work after only a few hours of sleep. It was a lot easier once I finally passed my driving test. It took me a while, mind. I didn't pass until my third attempt, which was so frustrating because I wanted to feel the same sense of freedom that I had when I'd learned to ride my bike all those years before. I wanted my independence so I didn't have to rely on anyone else.

The first time I took my test, the examiner was very stern and old-fashioned. He told me to go straight across the road in front of me, and I said, 'If I go straight across, I'm going to be going the wrong way around the bollards, and I'll be on the wrong side of the road.' He was insistent, so I did as he said, and I must have got things mixed up; I failed before I even left the test centre. My driving instructor was sitting in a café across the road watching it all, going, 'Aaargghhh! What the hell is she doing?'

I had to finish the test, though, and I did everything else perfectly, but I still failed. The second time I took my test, I failed on several small things, but thankfully on the third time, I was handed my 'passed' certificate, and I was thrilled. I was so happy, I grabbed the examiner and kissed him on the cheek!

I bought my first car for £40. It was an old maroon Ford Anglia, so it wasn't the chicest-looking thing. It was fantastic – apart from the fact that it was in a right state and everything was conking out. But still, it got me to and from work every night. It served me well, and even though things kept going wrong, it didn't end up costing me that much over the next two years, so it was a good investment.

When I was driving to and from the nightclubs, I'd often pick up my friend Sue. My window wipers had packed up at the time, and I couldn't afford to get them fixed.

The car had small triangular windows, and if it was raining, Sue had to stick her arm out of the window on her side and use a long-handled umbrella to wipe the rain off the windshield. I'm not sure it was terribly safe, but you could get away with it in those days!

Another time, my handbrake broke, so my brother had to come in the car with me, and if I stopped on a hill, he had to run out and put a brick behind one of the back wheels to stop it rolling backwards.

I must have been a good driver to handle all of that! I had a lot of fun in that car, and I felt like a proper grown-up when I was driving. When I finally got a new car, I gave the Anglia to my sister Angela's husband, Tommy, and he had it for another couple of years. Sure, it was a potential death trap, but it got you from A to B!

These days, I drive a Bentley and a Porsche 911. I would never, in my wildest dreams, have imagined that I would one day have enough money to buy a decent car, let alone the ones I've got. But I'll never forget my driving roots. That Anglia will be in my heart forever.

CHAPTER TWO

To Love Somebody

Not long after I started singing with the Dixies, I met the man who would go on to become my husband. I knew Robert was the man for me the minute I laid eyes on him. I was on stage rehearsing a song, and the floor had just been waxed by this big machine, so he skidded across the floor and stood in front of me to try and get my attention. It was so funny.

He was so handsome – I thought he looked like Warren Beatty – and he still is. The only problem was, he was the under-manager of the club, so we had to hide the fact that we were dating. My manager Ronnie didn't allow us to have boyfriends, which was quite common for female club singers back then. It's a bit like how boy bands always pretend they don't have girlfriends. We had to look like we were available.

Robert is very kind and gentle, and he's also very good at business, although I didn't see that side of him until later on. I just thought he was gorgeous, and that was enough for me in the early days. He was my first serious boyfriend, and, to be honest, I liked it that way. I hadn't been in any rush to meet someone and have a proper relationship before I met him, because I was too busy working and being with my family. For some reason, though, when I met him, I suddenly felt ready. Maybe I'd been waiting for a special man to come along who I would want to make space in my life for?

My father was a bit worried about me dating someone that worked in the club, but as soon he met Robert, he realised he didn't have anything to worry about. It was obvious he would look after me.

I loved working at the Townsman, and I wanted to do more shifts because I was earning more singing there than I was ever going to at the shop. I didn't want to give up my job at the grocery, though, because I never thought I'd be able to make a career out of working in the clubs. I thought it was just a flash in the pan and could end any minute, so I needed a steady income just in case anything happened. I spoke to Ronnie Williams about working a few more evenings a week, and he asked me if I could manage six nights out of seven with Tuesdays off. Without even pausing for breath, I said yes. I used to work from 9am until 5pm in the shop, go home and have some dinner, get changed and then work from 8pm until 1am in the Townsman. I felt so lucky to be in the Dixies, and I didn't mind working as much as I did. I'd also persuaded my younger sister, Avis, to audition to become a Dixie because she had a very soulful voice. She passed with flying colours, so we got to hang out all the time.

I was only eighteen, so you would think I had loads of energy and would be able to keep up that kind of schedule, but I am terrible in the mornings, and I always have been. I was always trying to catch up on sleep. Somehow, I managed to stick to that timetable for about eighteen months, but I can't imagine trying to do that now. I've never been a morning person; I'm much more of a night owl, and I don't seem to get tired when I'm doing shows. I think the buzz of it all gives me energy.

I was getting bored working in the grocery, and Marlene told me some jobs were going in a confectionery warehouse called Jenkins, where she worked. I applied for a job there and handed in my notice at the grocery as soon as I got it. It was fabulous working at Jenkins, because Marlene and I became closer than ever. She had moved out of home years ago after getting married, so it was wonderful spending so much time with her again.

I'm surprised I wasn't the size of a house working there. If a box of sweets broke coming down the packing conveyor, the company weren't able to sell them, so we used to share the sweets between us.

Jenkins had a second warehouse nearby where my sister Angela worked in the office. Meanwhile, my brother Lynn drove the Jenkins vans to drop off deliveries, so it was a proper family affair. Back when I had still been at school, Lynn would sometimes let me go on afternoon runs around the valleys with him, and I thought it was so exciting to see life outside of Skewen.

Somehow, Robert and I were able to hide our relationship for about a year, but when the manager eventually found out, he told me I couldn't work in the Townsman anymore, which is ridiculous because it hadn't interfered with our work at all. Still, he said it set a bad example, so he got me a job in a hotel nearby called The Redcliff in Caswell Bay. I was really pissed off about it, because I loved the Townsman!

I sang with a jazz band at The Redcliff, so I tried to make myself feel better because at least I was learning some new singing skills. I worked there off and on for about a year, and then Bobby Wayne and the Dixies moved to another club called The Showboat and asked me to start working with them again. I was thrilled. We also worked in a club called The Melody quite regularly, so we moved around a bit. There were so many clubs around back then, and some famous artists coming down to do shows, like Marty Wilde and Tony Christie. Sometimes they would do a week-long run, and we would get to watch them while we were on our break or having dinner, which was usually chicken or scampi in a basket. I hadn't met any famous people before, so to have bands I'd heard on the radio standing right in front of me was quite something. I learned a lot from watching the way they sang and moved. If they had taught that in school, I definitely would have paid attention!

In the end, I had to give up my job at Jenkins, because it was impossible to keep up with that crazy schedule – and I was earning good money in the clubs, so I didn't have to worry about being able to afford my false eyelashes. Robert and I were going from strength to strength and life felt good; almost perfect.

One night, I borrowed Robert's car to get to one of the clubs. I loved driving it because it was such a cool car. Robert had a convertible E-Type Jag, which was a bit different to driving the Anglia. I drove the car to The Showboat in the Mumbles with my friend and fellow Dixie, Sue. I parked perfectly and put the crook lock on to keep the car safe.

When I finished my shift at about 1.30am, Sue and I returned to the car. I must have been a bit tired, because instead of undoing the crook lock, I stepped over it. I had also put it around the brake instead of the accelerator. To this day, I have no idea why.

I started up the car, and it rolled forward. When I went to put my foot on the brake, the crook lock was in the way, so there was no way of stopping the car. It kept moving forward – and, of course, I was parked right in front of a lamppost. I went straight into it, and we heard the most horrendous crunching sound. The light at the top of the lamppost fell on to Robert's beautiful car, and Sue and I screamed. We were cowering in case it bounced and came through the windscreen. Thank goodness E-Types have such long bonnets, because it meant the light didn't come through the soft top. Instead, it crashed on to the ground while the post swayed around in front of us. We had a *really* lucky escape there.

Eventually, I got the crook lock off, and I drove straight to the Townsman. Robert was working, and as I drove around the roundabout next to the club, some of his friends were standing outside. I could see one of them mouthing, 'Oh my god, look! Look at the state of the car!' The grill was all bent up, and it looked awful. Robert was amazingly calm about it, I have to say. I'm not sure I would have been!

*

In 1971, I was asked to go to London to audition to be a backing singer on Lou Christie's tour. It was the first time I'd ever been to London, and it was like a whole new world. As I mentioned before, even places like Swansea and Cardiff seemed huge to me, so when I got to London, I thought, *Wow! What a place!*

Lou was lovely, but he said to me, 'I love your voice – but you don't dance or anything, do you?'

'No,' I replied. 'I'm a singer!'

39

Sadly, he wanted someone who could do both. While I was disappointed at the time, fate clearly had other plans for me.

In those days, Robert also worked six days a week, and he took Tuesdays off too, so we could spend some time together in the evening. We'd see each other during the day, and then we would be working in the clubs at night. By the time we finished work, the only restaurants that were still open were either the Indian or the Chinese, so we used to alternate. Then every Tuesday, we would go to the Berni Inn on the high street in Swansea.

I suppose, given how often we were in Indian restaurants, it was quite fitting that Robert got down on one knee and proposed to me in our favourite one, The Kismet, in September 1972. He bought me a solitaire diamond ring from a goldsmith in Swansea, and then in 1978, when he had a bit more money, he bought me a larger diamond to replace it. I still keep the original one in a box, and every now and again I'll have a look at it and smile, remembering that night.

The funny thing about Robert that not many people know is that he was famous several years before I was. He was a British judo champion, and he got his third Dan black belt in judo when he was only nineteen. He was always in the papers back then, so people knew who he was way before they'd heard of some Welsh singer called Bonnie Tyler!

In 1970, a month after we got engaged, Robert went to live and train in Japan for eight months in preparation for the 1972 Olympics in Munich, West Germany. He had already taken part in lots of competitions, and he was a reigning European bronze champion.

While he was away, we tried to keep in touch by sending airmail letters. They were these envelopes made of very thin paper that opened up into a large letter. We used to write to each other every single day, but there was a six-week postal strike at the time, so nothing was coming through. You can imagine how hard it is to write every day when you know someone isn't going to get your letters, but I still wrote them because when he finally got them, I wanted him to know that I was thinking about him and supporting him. At the end of the strike, six weeks' worth of letters came through my door, and it took me days to read them all. I've still got bundles of them in a box at home.

In 1972, Robert represented the UK in the Olympics. In the Olympic Village, all the countries were put in different barracks, arranged very close to each other. I remember turning on the telly one night, and it was headline news that eight members of a Palestinian militant organisation called Black September had stormed one of the barracks and killed two members of the Israeli Olympics team. Nine other members of the team were taken as hostages.

It was a very scary time for anyone who had relatives out there, especially as it was almost impossible to get information about what was going on. All we knew was that there was gunfire and people had been killed. I was so scared for Robert. Mobile phones didn't exist, and I didn't have a phone in the house. Even if I went to a phone box, I had no idea of how I could get hold of Robert, and he had no way of contacting me. My mind was telling me all sorts of things because we didn't know all the ins and outs of what had happened. The news was being drip-fed to us as and when the TV stations had more information, so we didn't have a proper overview of what was going on. It was terrifying.

I was glued to the TV, praying that Robert was okay. When the Olympics kicked off, I sat with my friend Christine and her mother and father, because I couldn't watch it alone. I was on tenterhooks as the British team walked out – and then all of a sudden, I saw Robert looking healthy and well.

He competed in the men's welterweight event, and while he didn't win a medal, he had already beaten his Russian opponent Kachenko a few times previously. I think he was a bit disappointed, but out of all the British judo experts in the country, he was one of only six in the team, so he was also very proud of himself for getting that far. Olympic competitors weren't paid in those days either, so he'd had to work hard and pay for everything himself. I was so proud of him, too, and very happy when he finally arrived home.

We got married in 1973 when I was twenty-two and he was twenty-four. At that time, I was still living at home with my parents, and Robert was living with his grandfather. His mother died when he was eight, so his grandparents brought him and his brother Michael up while his father was working. Eight years later, his father got married again, to Gwen, and Michael went to live with Gwen and his father. But Robert lived with his grandparents until we moved in together.

It was a beautiful wedding. We got married in Skewen, in the same church where Marlene and Gwyn, and Lynn and Margaret, had also got married. Every christening we've had has been there too.

I couldn't expect my mother and father to pay for a big wedding when they had so many of us, and neither of them were working at the time. Robert and I did it all between us, and I paid for my dress and flowers and a car. It was all very traditional, but that's how we wanted it. I had lots of bridesmaids, flower girls and page boys, and the most wonderful reception. When I look back at the photos now, I think my hair was a bit too blonde and curly, but aside from that, it was a perfect day.

We had the reception in the Townsman. Luckily, we got a deal, so it was much cheaper than it would usually be. By today's standards, it would cost an arm and a leg to have the wedding we had, but Robert had all the catering done by the Townsman staff, and he even helped Vito, the Italian chef, cook the food for the turkey dinners. It was one of the most amazing days of my life. Everyone wants their wedding to go perfectly, and I really did feel like mine was everything I hoped it would be.

*

I loved being in the Dixies, but I was getting more and more confident, and I wanted to push myself even further. I wanted to be a singer with my own band. I put out some feelers looking for musicians, and within a week, we had a fully-formed band. Ronnie had left by then, and he was no longer managing me now I'd left the Dixies, so we went back to my favourite spot.

I teamed up with musicians Robert Grinter, Kevin Dunne and Mike Adams. We called ourselves Imagination, and we soon became the resident band in the Townsman.

I became the main singer, and I would do lead vocals and harmonise with the band. We worked six days a week, once again only taking Tuesdays off. We used to fit two forty-five-minute slots in at weekends too, mainly in working men's clubs and Conservative and Labour clubs. We played all over the place and were making quite good money. We played all kinds of music: a lot of songs that were in the charts at the time, along with everything from country to rock to old-time dancing songs on a Sunday. We used to perform waltzes and bossa novas – songs people could dance to in their ballroom outfits.

When I was twenty-four, Imagination and I applied and got accepted to go on a TV programme called *New Faces*, which younger readers may not have heard of! It was a bit like a very early version of *Britain's Got Talent*, but without the big budget.

We performed a song called 'Armed and Extremely Dangerous', which was originally released by an American band called First Choice. Mickie Most, a very well-known record producer, was one of the judges on the panel. He was the Simon Cowell-type figure. He said to us, 'The girl's got something, but the band is just playing away.'

So that was the end of us.

My sister Avis also went on *New Faces* and won her heat! She went on to make it to the final. She was up against a male singer, and again, it was Mickie Most who scuppered her chances by giving one more point to the man. If it hadn't been for that, she would have won the whole competition that season. You can find her song, 'Lies', on YouTube under the name Amanda Paul. She's beautiful, and she's got the most amazing, soulful voice.

Avis got a record deal, but in the end it didn't work out for her that way, although she did have a great passion for it. I believe that she was made to be an amazing mother, which she is – and she's now a fantastic grandmother as well. We've all got our own paths to follow, and her life was supposed to go in a different direction. She's got beautiful children and grandchildren, and that's what makes her glow. I think that was her destiny, and it's what makes her happier than anything. She doesn't regret a thing about not taking her career further because, for whatever reason, it didn't feel right. She still sings to this day, but she sings with the church band for charities.

*

In 1974, I was still performing in clubs and married to Robert. I had a happy life with my family and friends, and I was doing the thing I loved as a job. I wondered how life could get any better, to be honest.

Did I regret not getting the job with Lou Christie, and not getting further on *New Faces*? Maybe a bit, but I had a lovely set-up back home, and maybe it just wasn't the right time. People say things happen for a reason, and I've found that to be true a lot in my life. People also often say that I'm one of life's lucky ones, and that I always seem to be in the right place at the right time. Things have somehow worked out for me – in the strangest of ways. Not that I'm complaining, mind.

One of the greatest examples of that has to be when Roger Bell, who was a talent scout for Valley Music in London, came to the Townsman. He'd come to see his friend Victor Oakley, who was the resident singer upstairs at the club. They worked together in the 1960s with a band called the

Bystanders. Funnily enough, Victor lived in the council house opposite mine with his grandmother, or Granny Broad, as she was known, when we were growing up. Even though he was a fair bit older than me, we knew each other quite well. When I was young and singing into a hairbrush in my bedroom, he'd already been on tour in Germany with his band and played at lots of different venues. I used to get private concerts, because they often rehearsed on his granny's front lawn.

Roger had come down to potentially sign him. That was the norm back then; if a record company got word of a good act, they'd send someone to check them out. I find it fascinating that these days people get discovered on YouTube and social media and all sorts. It's probably easier to get yourself noticed these days, but I'm not sure it's any easier to get signed to a record label. Mind you, a lot of these youngsters do it all themselves now. They put music out and promote it over Instagram, and they take charge of their own careers. They're so clever. The music business has changed so much since I started out.

I was at the Townsman the same night, performing on the ground floor with Imagination. That night, Roger happened to go to the wrong floor, and he saw me on stage singing Freda Payne's 'Band Of Gold'. For whatever reason, I stood out to him. Years later, he said, 'When I saw her, she was that different.' Roger didn't say anything to me at the time, so I had no idea who he was. I thought he was just another customer.

Roger went back to London and told a producer called Ronnie Scott (not the jazz musician!) all about me, then contacted me at the club and asked me if I was willing to go to London to record a demo song in a studio. Of course I was!

I had been to London several times by now, for the audition with Lou Christie and to buy stage outfits for the Dixies, but this was the first time I'd gone on my own, and it was a big deal. My mother was worried about me and told me to be careful – she was always on at me to be careful – and I promised her I would.

I was twenty-five and married by then, so I wasn't a kid, but it still felt quite scary. I had to travel from Swansea to Paddington station. The train used to run right along the back of our house, so my mother always used to ask what train I was getting, and she and my little brother and sister would wave from the bedroom window as the train went by. I used to get up out of my seat and go to the carriage window, and I'd wave back at them.

When I arrived at Paddington, Roger Bell came and met me and took me to RG Jones Studio in Morden, south London, in a black cab. David Mackay was there with Ronnie Scott, as well as two guys called Alan Tarney and Trevor Spencer. They were in the Tarney/Spencer Band, and also wrote for Cliff Richard.

It was my first time being in that environment, and it was a wonderful experience. In those days, the desks were enormous, with all these switches and lights everywhere. It's crazy to think that these days, you can make music on your computer in your bedroom. (Well, I couldn't, but clever techy people can!)

David paid for the session that day, so I could do the demo while Alan and Trevor performed the backing track. David then took the recording around to record labels and agents in the hope of getting me a record deal. No one bit. So I thought that was probably the end of that.

I went back home and carried on singing in the clubs, and life went back to normal. I didn't hear anything from Ronnie Scott for months and months, and I had accepted that it was dead in the water. I felt like it would have been amazing if something had come of the demo, but I certainly hadn't pinned all my hopes on it working out. I had a lovely life back home, so it wasn't as if I was sitting in my bedroom every night hoping I would get a phone call or letter that would change everything. I've always been a 'what will be, will be' kind of person, and I've always thought that what is meant for you won't pass you by.

These days, you can become famous for posting videos of yourself doing funny things or wearing lovely clothes or showing people how to put on make-up, but back in the seventies, the only ways to get famous were to become a singer, an actress or a presenter. They were the real stars.

I didn't ever feel that pull or desperation to be famous; I just loved singing. I'd had such a solid upbringing, and I always had love around me, so I didn't suffer from a huge amount of self-doubt. We all have our moments of insecurity, of course, but I cracked on and let life take me where it wanted to.

*

Right from the start of our marriage, Robert was incredible with money. He didn't just work as the under-manager of the Townsman; he also used to earn extra money restocking the bars with drinks. He's always been a very hard worker and a very good saver, and he invested really wisely. As a result of that, we were able to buy our first bungalow in Llansamlet almost as soon as we got married. It was brand new when we moved in because Robert bought it off-plan. I put about £2,000 towards it, and Robert paid the rest, so we didn't even have a mortgage.

We lived in that bungalow for about two years, and then Robert bought a plot of land in Mumbles, which is a lovely place. It's so beautiful there; it's got some wonderful shops, and it's right on the sea. The Gower Coast is stunning, and a lot of holidaymakers visit because it's so charming. He had a house built for us, and we lived in it very happily for sixteen years – aside from a horrible incident that happened just after we'd moved in that still haunts me to this day.

Robert and I were travelling home together at around 2.30am. As we walked up to the front door, Robert said to me, 'Oh god, I can hear water dripping. You didn't leave the water on, did you?'

I knew I hadn't, but I kept thinking, *Did I? Could I have done?*

Robert went in first, and there was water pouring through the ceilings. We'd had brand-new carpets laid throughout the house just two days before, and they were proper seventies white shagpile carpets as well. We also had brand-new furniture and a new kitchen, and all the walls had been freshly painted. You name it, we'd got it. And it was all ruined.

Some people had broken in and completely trashed the place. Believe it or not, this was on Christmas Eve, of all times. You wouldn't believe the damage they had done. They had broken Robert's awards and pulled the handles off his trophies. They'd kicked over the Christmas tree and trashed all the presents. They threw paint over our new furniture, they slashed all our clothes, and they put plugs in all the sinks and baths and turned on the water. They even turned the fridge freezer upside down, with all the Christmas food in it. We hadn't even had time to put the curtains up – so at least they weren't ruined.

The house was in quite a secluded place, which is why none of the neighbours heard or saw anything. We called the police, but there wasn't much they could do because this was in the days before CCTV. The police said they thought there must have been six or seven of them to do all that damage, though.

We couldn't sleep there, of course, so one of Robert's friends let us stay at his house. We didn't want to have to go to my mother and father's at that time of the morning.

The next day, we were expected at my parents' house for lunch. At first, we didn't tell anyone about what had happened because it was Christmas Day and we didn't want to ruin it. My mother picked up on it, though, and asked what the matter was. I broke down and told them everything. They comforted us and said they would do whatever they could to help. We went to live with my mother and father for four months while all the damage was being sorted out. By then, all my brothers and sisters had left home, so there was plenty of room for us, and they treated us so well.

We did get over it, but it was heartbreaking at the time.

We never found out who did it, but Robert had his suspicions. That afternoon, a gang of ruffians had tried to get into the Townsman, and he'd refused them entry. As they walked away, one of them had said to him, 'We'll have you, Sullivan.' We couldn't prove anything, but whoever it was obviously planned it, because they took spray cans and tins of paint along with them. They planned to do as much damage as possible, and believe me, they did. I don't think they could have done anything worse unless they had burned the house down.

The absolute worst moment for me was when our poor dog came running up to us, covered in different coloured paints. The bastards had spray-painted him. He was absolutely terrified and shaking all over, and that upset me more than anything. He was such a sweet boy, and it broke my heart to see him like that.

He was a Jack Russell called Sam and had been my husband's grandfather's dog. Robert's mother died when he was eight, so he was brought up by his grandparents, and when his grandfather passed, he wanted to make sure Sam had a good home. Sam lived with Robert's brother Michael for a while, but when we went to visit him one day, the little dog jumped in the back of the car. We realised it was because he missed Robert, so he ended up coming home with us.

We had him for eight years after that. He was jet black and very handsome, but he was also a real barker, and he was always chasing the postman. He sounded like he would be vicious, but he was such a friendly little chap.

The thing with dogs is that they become such a big part of your family. Every time we came home, he ran up to greet us, but he was also very happy being on his own. He was able to go in and out of the garden, and sometimes we'd come home and find him sitting on the front doorstep, waiting for us.

A couple of years later, when I had my first hit record and started touring, my mother and father would take care of Sam. They loved him. When he passed away, we didn't think it was fair to get another dog while we were still travelling so much. My mother and father were getting older, and it wouldn't have been right to rely on them. I'd love to have a dog now, but I still travel so much that it would be hard on them – and us. I'll have to make do with stroking other people's, and my fond memories of little Sam.

*

One day, completely out of the blue, two years after I'd recorded the demo in London, Ronnie Scott contacted me through Roger, and sent me some songs to learn: 'My! My! Honeycomb', 'I've Got So Used to Loving You, Baby', 'Lost in France' and 'Baby I Remember You'. They asked me to send them a tape of me singing them so they could see if the songs suited my voice.

Thankfully, they thought they did, so we agreed we'd record the demos in a proper studio. I was shocked but over the moon, and I was soon heading back to London to do a recording session. David told me he had a deal with RCA Records to find three new acts for their roster, and he wanted me to be one of them, along with Digby Richards and a group called Buster. I was twenty-six by then, which seems very old compared to modern-day pop stars, who often start in their teens.

I wore a little crocheted mini-dress that my cousin Dorothy had made for me, and I felt very overwhelmed, especially when I discovered that Ronnie had written 'Jesamine' by the Casuals, which was one of my favourite songs from the sixties. He had also written 'Ice in the Sun' for Status Quo and 'I'm a Tiger' for Lulu, so that made me even more nervous. What if I was utter crap?

Thankfully, it went brilliantly, and once the demos were recorded, David was ready to take them to RCA – but not before Ronnie insisted on changing my stage name. He said Shereen sounded like a belly dancer's name and asked me to come up with something else.

I looked through a load of newspapers and made a list of first names and surnames. Then I put them together to see what worked. Steven Tyler from Aerosmith must have been in the paper that day, because I named myself after him. I'd always loved the name Bonnie, and they seemed to fit together well, so my new alter ego was created. I still like the name to this day, so I think I did a pretty good job.

I will always be Gaynor to my friends and family, and I find it easy to separate Gaynor from Bonnie. I'm Gaynor at home and Bonnie on stage. People who don't know me well call me Bonnie all the time, but that's to be expected, and I don't mind a bit.

At times, it felt like the possibility of getting a record deal was so close but also *so* far away. There were loads of great singers around; who was to say they would want me? If they had other female singers on their label, I might not be right for them. It was a painful wait to find out if my songs were going to be released or not. Still, I had never, ever expected to be recording songs in a studio, let alone get a contract, so I remained grateful for how far I'd got.

We didn't have a phone at home in those days, but there was a phone box near my house. One of the neighbours always answered it and passed on messages, and one day they said I'd had a call from my management asking me to phone back as soon as possible. I didn't know if it was good or bad news from RCA, but at least now I'd find out one way or the other.

I nervously put my money into the phone and called my management's office. One of them – and I honestly can't remember who, because I was so excited – said to me, 'We've done it! We've got a record deal for you with RCA. They said yes!' Well, you could have knocked me down with a feather. People like me didn't get record deals or release singles, and yet that was exactly what I would be doing. I was so excited. I couldn't believe it. I was signing to Elvis Presley's record label! Signing on the dotted line was a special moment, if not a slightly surreal one. I just remember grinning like mad, and afterwards, Ronnie, David, Steve and I had a celebratory hug. The three of them became my creative and management team, which was very reassuring because I knew them and liked them a lot. I felt safe knowing they would be looking out for me. I had an inkling the music industry could be quite cut-throat.

It was decided that one of the songs we'd recorded for the demo, 'My! My! Honeycomb', would be my first release on RCA Records. It was a lovely song written by Jimmy Luck and John Szego. The B-side was 'I've Got So Used to Loving You' by Jack Gellar, which was Ronnie Scott's pseudonym during the late sixties and early seventies.

No one knew who I was, so the only radio station that

played my single was Swansea Sound. My brother Lynn made posters and put them up in shop windows around our village to let people know that my first single was coming out, but it wasn't *quite* enough to score me a hit! Even though I think everyone I'd ever known bought a copy, it still wasn't enough to crack the top forty.

I felt disappointed, but my management team assured me it didn't mean my career was over before it had started. It was quite normal for new artists to release several tracks before they found one that resonated with the public and became a hit. I had signed a five-year deal with RCA, and they were pushing for me to release another song as soon as possible.

RCA insisted that 'Lost in France' should be the next single. It wasn't really 'me', because it was quite a pretty song, and I was always doing the rockier tracks during my residencies. It didn't feel like the type of song I wanted to sing or the image I wanted to create for myself, but my managers told me to trust them, and I did, implicitly, so I went with it. Everyone seemed to think it would be a hit, and I suppose it grew on me in the end. It's a catchy song, and the more I heard it, the more I liked it, even if I still wasn't 100 per cent convinced about it.

Back then, you recorded on to big machine tapes and then you had to cut them and splice them, so it was much more complicated than it is now. They had already recorded the music for 'Lost in France', so all I had to do was go in and put my voice on the track, so it sounded much more professional than the demo versions had.

Ronnie Scott and David Mackay were joint producers on the song, while Steve Wolfe was one of the songwriters and also did backing vocals. Even though I liked 'My! My! Honeycomb', when I was recording 'Lost in France', I felt like it had something different about it that may appeal to people. It's very French-sounding, with the accordion and ukulele, so it was nice, and it was romantic. I knew it would appeal to a certain market.

RCA obviously felt the same because they put some really big promotion behind the single to get the word out there. Rodney Birback, the marketing director, invited fifty journalists, radio DJs and photographers to Heathrow Airport and told them to bring their passports. They had no idea where they were going, but once they arrived, they were told they were being flown to Le Touquet airport in France. There were leaflets in the pockets of every seat on the plane saying, 'Could we be lost in France?'

Meanwhile, I was being flown to Toulouse in a small private plane so that I'd be there when everyone arrived. It won't come as any surprise to hear that it was the first time I had ever been on a private plane. I felt so special. Robert and I used to go on package holidays to Spain, so I was used to great big planes packed with loads of people.

The press were driven to a chateau, and they were all handed a bio explaining who I was, as well as a single of 'Lost in France' and a note that said, 'We hope you're enjoying being lost in France.' For someone who wasn't used to the way the music business works, it was quite a shock to be the centre of something so spectacular.

I never wore many dresses, and I still don't. But that day, I needed to wear something that was in keeping with the song, so I wore a flowery, silky off-the-shoulder dress. I guess it was the image the record company wanted to put across. I was only twenty-six, and I was tottering around the chateau grounds in this dress with high heels, pretending it was the kind of thing I wore every day.

In the middle of the main hall, there was a long table, and all the guests were sitting around it, being served this incredible lunch. It was all a bit embarrassing, though, because every course was brought up to me for approval before it was served, and I was *dying*. I didn't know anything about French food; I was much more familiar with Indian, Chinese and Italian dishes. I decided the best thing to do was to keep smiling and nodding my head every time another platter of fish or meat was presented to me. I'm no Gordon Ramsay, and I didn't even know what some of the dishes were.

Once everyone had finished eating, they were free to wander around the beautiful grounds while I did loads of one-on-one interviews and had photographs taken. The interviews were nerve-wracking, because it was all so new. I was always second-guessing myself, thinking, *Am I being interesting enough? What if they ask me something I don't know the answer to?* But I have to say, everyone was so lovely to me that day. The wine they served with lunch may have helped!

I've never been one to answer personal questions. I decided that very early on. I always said, 'If you want to ask questions about my career, that's fine, but I like to keep my personal life to myself.' I guess it was instinctive. I never had any media training like a lot of artists do now. I didn't know how to avoid hard questions or make my answers interesting. I had just always felt like my private life was my own, and there was no need to share everything. I thought the music was far more interesting anyway. The number of times George Michael was hounded, and things were written about him, and yet he was making these incredible albums. *That's* what they should have been writing about. It's none of their bloody business if someone prefers someone of their own sex, or the opposite sex, or both! They shouldn't be allowed to ask personal things like that. If someone wants to tell the press, that's fine, but no one should ever feel pressured into anything. You know, you look at someone like Adam Lambert, and he's very happy to talk about his sexuality, but that's his choice, and he hasn't been pushed into it.

My father always used to say to me, 'Stay away from religion and politics, because you can't win,' and I've always followed that advice. You can't do right for doing wrong, and you will always offend someone. I do believe in God, and I know that I've been blessed in my life, but that's as far as I'll go. I don't say a word about politics.

I would say the most open I've ever been is in this book. This is the most in-depth I've ever gone – but that's very different, because it's on my terms. There is a lot I want to share that I would never have dreamed of talking about twenty years ago. This just feels like the right time.

I was lucky because, from day one, I managed to separate my private life from my work life. I'd be performing a show to a huge crowd in Germany one day, and then sitting down for dinner with Robert or my mother and father and watching TV the following night. I didn't ever struggle with the two worlds crossing over, and I feel so blessed for that.

I was never into the rock'n'roll lifestyle. I love rock music, but I'm hardly the type who's going to throw a TV out of a hotel room window, am I? I think the most outrageous thing

I've ever done was during an interview with a rock critic in Denmark. He was convinced my hair was a wig, and he grabbed it and tried to pull it off. It wasn't a wig, so it bloody hurt! I don't know what made me do it, but I was so angry I grabbed him by the balls and said, 'Are *yours* real?' My mother would have really told me off for that.

*

The chateau event turned out to be a really good investment; it truly helped to put me on the map. Everybody had such a great time. The journalists wrote about it in their magazines and newspapers, and DJs put 'Lost in France' on their play-lists. I mean, if the song had been total rubbish, no one would have played it anyway, but it was about getting it into the right hands so people actually heard it.

In those days, DJs and members of the press got sent hundreds of different records every week, and there was no way they could listen to them all. You had to try and stand out, and that's what that day in France was for. It introduced me to so many new people, and they got to know what I was all about.

I think the fact that my voice was a bit different to other female singers helped too. When you heard a Dusty Springfield song, for example, you knew it was her instantly, and the record company were hoping the same would be true with me because I had this unique, husky sound (although it got a lot huskier further down the line, which we'll come to later).

The Radio 1 DJ Simon Bates was a huge supporter of mine, and he said, 'If this doesn't make it into the top ten, I'll scrub the steps of the BBC with a toothbrush.' Thankfully, his tooth-brush was safe, because 'Lost in France' just scraped into the top ten at number nine.

This was followed by number ones in other parts of Europe, like Germany and Austria. The song was in the top ten for six months in Germany. I couldn't believe it. That's when my career really started.

My friends and family were so excited for me, and I don't think they could quite believe it. I was still based in Wales, so nothing had changed – apart from the fact that I had a hit single in the charts and was being flown all over Europe to do shows and interviews. Everyone close to me has always been so supportive of me, and I never lost touch with any of them or started to think I was something special. If I had, they would have brought me back down to earth with a bang!

I was interviewed by *Record Mirror* about the success of the single, and I said to them, 'It came as a bit of a surprise to have a hit record. I never really thought about it before. I'm enjoying it. I just like singing.' Thank goodness I did get better at doing interviews over the years.

Without a doubt, the best thing about 'Lost in France' being a hit was being invited to perform on *Top of the Pops*. This was a dream come true for me: performing on the programme I had loved for so long. When we got on stage, my bass player, Kevin Dunne, said to me, 'You've arrived! You're on *Top Of The Pops*!' and a shiver went up my spine.

In those days, you had a couple of hours in the afternoon to re-record a 'live' version of the song, and then you had to mime to it – you couldn't just go on and mime to the record.

It meant I was there for quite a lot of the day, trying to spot celebrities.

All these big artists were on the show in the same week as me, like ELO and Cliff Richard, as well as all the dancers I used to watch when I was a kid. I thought they were so cool and glamorous – and there I was, on the stage right next to them! In my mind, the dancers were much more famous than I was. My cousin and I dreamed of being a part of that world. And now, here I was.

My brother Paul was so excited I was going to be on the same show as Cliff Richard, and he asked me if I could get his autograph. Just as I'd built up the courage to ask him, the floor manager called him to the stage. Before he headed off, he turned and said, 'Bonnie, I'll happily do the autograph for your brother. Just make sure I get your address, and I'll post it to you.' Later on, I gave him my address, and he stayed true to his word and sent it to me. How fantastic is that?

For the performance, I wore a flared trouser suit I'd bought locally in Wales; I couldn't afford designer clothes or anything too fancy. I remember being very nervous about being on such a big show, and one that had shaped me so much during my younger years. I was always nervous when I had to do something new, but that was next level. I know I was stiff during my performance because I didn't know what I should be doing, so I made it as easy for myself as I could.

That first time being on *Top of the Pops* was incredibly special. I went to the BBC bar after the show, and I couldn't believe I was drinking in the same place as all these stars. It was a great atmosphere, and it felt like the coolest night out you could imagine. In those days, record companies were very flush, so they took me and the band out for a meal to celebrate once we'd finished drinking!

As time went on and I made more appearances on *Top of the Pops*, I got to know the schedule. As soon as you got off stage, you went to the bar for a few drinks and then headed out for dinner. Sometimes you would be in the same restaurants as the other artists, which was always nice, and the record company always picked up the tab, which was also nice.

Because the song was so successful, I started touring all over Europe, and that's when I had my first taste of what life on the road was all about. I watched my first appearance on *Top of the Pops* on a TV set in a room at a Glasgow Airport hotel before flying off somewhere or other. The second time I was on the show, I watched it at home with all the family, including my excited aunts and uncles. It was lovely watching it with them, but also embarrassing. It had been my ultimate ambition to be on that show, and I remember having a moment when I thought, *Well, how the hell did that happen?*

*

As amazing as it was, I don't like seeing myself on TV very much. I'm always self-critical and think I could have done better.

Even now, if someone says something lovely, like I look good for my age, or whatever, I'll immediately say, 'Yes, but you should see me in the morning before I've got my make-up and lashes on and my hair done!' I won't even go to the shops without my make-up on. I don't feel good without my make-up. I envy people who have naturally dark eyelashes because they don't need any make-up, and mine are very fair.

I was a singer first and foremost, and I have never sold myself on trying to be sexy. I look at some of the girls who are in the charts now, and I think, 'Well, they've got nothing on!' I'm not judging, because people can do whatever they like, but if *Top of the Pops* was still on today, I'm not sure some of the artists would be allowed to wear so little!

People still phone me or message me now to tell me to put BBC2 on because they're showing an old episode of *Top of the Pops* with me on it. It is funny to see it again, and it brings back nothing but good memories. But I often think to myself, *Hmmm, that eyeshadow wasn't a good idea!* My father was right when he used to say to me, 'Those shoulder pads are far too big – you're making yourself look like an American football player!'

CHAPTER THREE

Getting So Exciting

The next single I released was called 'More Than a Lover'. It came out in January 1977. Ridiculously, it got banned from ITV for being too raunchy. A new teen pop show called *Get It Together* had launched at around the same time, and 'More Than a Lover' was put on a list of banned songs, along with Mr Big's top-five hit, 'Romeo'. Muriel Young, who was one of the main producers, thought my song was immoral because it contained the lyrics 'I wanted to be more than a lover'. She said, 'We have a duty to young viewers' parents and what they might read into the lyrics of the songs.' I don't think the lyrics were that saucy. The song was more about friendship and love than anything. It's crazy by today's standards, when you can get away with just about anything, but that's how it was in the seventies.

I thought Muriel's decision might do me a favour because it was free publicity and the music critics loved it, but because of the ban, it also failed to get any airplay from the BBC, and I wasn't invited to do any interviews with any of the major TV or radio stations, which was a big blow. The song reached number twenty-seven in the charts, which was still considered a hit, but it felt like a real let-down after the success of 'Lost in France'.

The funny thing is that many years later, Muriel ended up moving to Portugal, where Robert and I own a property, and her husband came and did the solar heating on our house. I remember saying to him, 'Your wife once banned my single from TV!', and we had such a good laugh about it. What are the chances of that? When people say it's a small world, they're not wrong.

Despite the 'More Than a Lover' disaster, shortly afterwards, we started working on my debut album in the Roundhouse Studios in London with some session musicians. Even though 'Lost in France' was a big hit, I secretly hoped it wasn't going to make it on to the album. I wanted a gutsier, rawer sound. I wasn't the sort to be wandering around cornfields looking wistfully into the distance while wearing floaty frocks. I wanted to move away from 'Lost in France' and go in a cooler direction. I saw it as more of a single than an album track, but of course, my managers and the record company wanted to include it so we could sell more copies, and I got it.

My first album came out on 3 February 1977. I called it *The World Starts Tonight* after one of the tracks on the album. It had ten songs on it in total, which were mainly written by Ronnie and Steve, but I also did a cover of 'Piece of My Heart' (because I loved Janis Joplin's version) and a version of Jerry Chesnut's 'Love of a Rolling Stone'.

I remember the shoot for that album cover; I sat astride a chair wearing jodhpurs. I look quite solemn in the photo because I didn't ever like to smile in pictures. I'm just not comfortable having my picture taken on shoots, you know. Even to this day, after all these years, I can't pose. I freeze in front of a camera, unless it's a natural situation like photos with friends and family.

*

To promote the album, I supported Gene Pitney on his UK tour, which meant I got to play at the London Palladium for the first time. It's such a special place, and there's so much history in there. Walking in and out of the stage door feels iconic, and the dressing rooms are battered and lived-in. I always think, *If these walls could talk . . .*

I was brought up watching shows like *Sunday Night at the London Palladium* because we loved Beat the Clock, and it felt like a million miles from our little village. When you find yourself on that stage, it's just wonderful to know you're standing on the same wooden boards all these megastars have been on. My mother and father came to that first performance, and they loved it. The idea that their little girl was going to be singing on that famous stage was something I don't think they could get their heads around until they saw me do it.

I wanted to make it really special for them, so before the show, I hired a limo to take them around and see all the sights of London – you know, Buckingham Palace and the Houses of Parliament and all that – and we all stayed at the Athenaeum Hotel near Hyde Park.

I had a private party for my friends and family in the bar upstairs after the show, and it was one of those 'pinch myself' moments, seeing everyone so happy. They had the absolute time of their lives.

I also played at Wolverhampton's Civic Hall and Aberdeen Capitol while I was supporting Gene, but I didn't have an awful lot to do with him. On the occasions I did speak to him, he was very nice and polite, but he was quite a shy man and he kept himself to himself. Someone told me that when he was staying in hotels, he never came out of his room. I couldn't quite understand why at first, but I guess he was so popular everybody wanted a piece of him, and he wasn't the kind of person that lapped up all the attention. He really came alive when he was on stage, though.

I can empathise with how he felt to a certain extent, because this business can be claustrophobic at times. If you're naturally quite insular, I can imagine it's much, much worse. The only time I've felt very overwhelmed was when I performed on a cruise ship. The singing part of it was great, because I went through all these secret corridors to get to the stage, but during the day, there was nowhere you could get away. When you're on a ship full of people, you can't perform and then go home. You're stuck onboard until it docks again.

As I've said before, I'm always happy to stop and chat with people and have pictures taken, but it was impossible even to go for a drink. It took Robert and I half an hour to make our way to the bar because so many people stopped us on the way. I tried to go shopping one day, but I didn't manage to buy anything because I was too busy doing selfies with people. I don't think I was used to that level of intensity; I am someone who needs to recharge my batteries after being around a lot of people, and there is no escape on a ship! I had a wonderful suite with a private deck so we spent most of our time in there, but I did feel a bit trapped, if I'm being honest.

*

'Lost in France' had sold over 250,000 copies, 'More Than a Lover' had made the headlines and my album was doing well. However, not everything was going smoothly in my life.

Not long after I supported Gene, I started to get a sore throat because all the singing I was doing was taking its toll. When I went to see a doctor, he discovered that I had nodules on my vocal cords. I'd had nodules three times before when I was singing in the clubs, and they went away with rest, but this time they kept coming back, faster and faster. In the end, my doctor said the only option was for them to be surgically removed.

I went in for the operation to have the nodules scraped off (I know, awful) at a private hospital in Bridgend in Wales. After the procedure, I was told by my surgeons not to talk, let alone sing, for six weeks. I had to write down what I wanted to say instead of talking, so everything took so bloody long. I was so frustrated because all I wanted to do was move forward with my career, but I couldn't sing, and I had to turn down all requests for interviews.

I had to carry a pen and paper everywhere, along with a sign I'd made that said, 'Sorry I can't talk to you, I've had a throat operation.' People probably thought, *She's had one hit record and she's got all above herself.*

In the end, I decided it was easier to stay in most of the time rather than have to see people and explain what had happened. But then I had another problem: I was so bored being stuck in the house, I couldn't stop eating, and I put on loads of weight. There was nothing else to do but watch TV and eat! Thankfully the weight did come off eventually.

One day, while I was on vocal rest, I drove my mother to visit my brother Lynn, who was in hospital. He'd had an accident and hurt his leg, so we went to cheer him up. As we were driving, I remembered that I'd forgotten to bring the strawberries and cream we'd bought for him, so I pulled over and wrote my mother a note asking if she had remembered them. She looked horrified and said, 'No, I forgot too!'

I was so frustrated that I'd have to drive all the way back home, I let out an 'Oh no!' scream. When I went for a check-up with the specialist a few days later, he used a bright light to check the back of my throat and then asked me if I'd been talking. I wrote down that I hadn't, which was half true. I had only let a few words – and one big scream – slip out.

He looked at me sternly and said, 'Well, it's too late now. You could have done permanent damage. I don't know what you've done, but there's nothing more we can do.'

My throat was supposed to clear up after six weeks, but it was a seemingly never-ending three months before I could sing at all. Even then, I sounded pretty terrible. There were moments when I was really scared I would never be able to sing in tune again, and I was devastated. I thought my chart career was done with. There was a possibility I'd never get my voice back, which I guess was my punishment for not sticking to the rules. Robert was a huge support and comfort to me if I was worried, and my family were amazing too. I didn't ever cry over it because I wanted to stay as positive as possible, but I did have some concerns that I wouldn't be able to sing again.

In July 1977, while I was on throat rest, RCA released another single from my album, called 'Heaven in July'. They didn't want people to forget about me, so they really got behind the track and even took out an advert in one of the big newspapers that said:

HEAVEN . . . if hearing's believing . . .

Remember 'Lost in France'? Remember how a lady called Bonnie Tyler caught the nation by the ears and catapulted the song into the top five? Remember how the style broadened, hardened with 'More Than a Lover'? How could this delicate, blue-eyed, butter-haired lady belt it out like a latter-day Janis Joplin? It's called talent. And right now, it's at a premium, but you'll find it on Bonnie's new single, 'Heaven'. Find out for yourself. Sit down. Put it on the deck and just . . . listen.

I found it hilarious. *Butter-haired*? Where did that come from?

Everything felt like it could be heading in the right direction again, but then tragically, Elvis died on 16 August, and it was like the world shifted. It was such a sad time. He was only forty-two, which is so young. When you're a kid, anyone over about twenty seems old, but once you hit middle age, you still feel like a kid yourself, and it's heartbreaking to think of what he missed out on.

It goes to show that all the success and money in the world can't bring you peace. You can kid yourself it will when you're younger because everything is fun and exciting, but when reality kicks in and you turn to drink or drugs to deal with your problems, you're fighting a losing battle. Elvis had everything so many people strive for in life, but I guess you could say, 'Be careful what you wish for.'

He was obviously struggling with fame, and you do wonder who was looking after him. It makes me realise how lucky I've been with the people who have managed me during my career, and also relieved that I've never been tempted to go down a self-destructive route.

Because Elvis was also signed to RCA, they went into overdrive trying to press copies of his back catalogue. There was a huge demand for Elvis's music, and they could barely keep up. That meant that every other artist on their roster was put on the back burner, including me. Sadly, with no other promotion behind me, aside from that rather strange poster, 'Heaven' only charted in Germany.

Once my throat *finally* healed and I was well enough to go back to work, I travelled to Surrey, where David Mackay had built his own studio. The plan was to do some record-ing with my touring band, who at that time were bassist Kevin Dunne, drummer Mike Gibbins (who played with Welsh rock band Badfinger), steel and rhythm guitarist Peter King, keyboard player Roger Bara and lead guitarist Taff Williams.

I started singing a new song called 'It's a Heartache' that Steve and Ronnie had written for me, and they said, 'Your voice has changed – it's gone all husky. But it's good; we like it!'

I'd always had quite a husky tone to my voice anyway, but as David joked, I now sounded like a female Rod Stewart! I was so flattered because I've always thought Rod is amazing. What a compliment!

We were all excited about getting the single out because it had a different sound, and I had a good feeling about it. When David, Ronnie and Steve took the song to RCA to get a release date, the head of A&R (Artist and Repertoire) said all the re-pressings of all Elvis's albums had pushed everything back, and they wouldn't be able to release the single for another eight months. *Eight months?* You're kidding me! Ten more new female singers could have released singles by then, and I'd be old news!

The guys were so gutted they called a meeting with Ken Clancy, the head of RCA, and said that if the record company weren't willing to release it sooner, they would challenge my contract with them. Ken listened to the track and immediately instructed the A&R team to release it the following week, on Friday 4 November.

'It's a Heartache' turned out to be a slow burner, but it eventually climbed to number four in the charts. I was in Germany on tour, and the BBC called my management because they wanted me to appear on *Top of the Pops* that week. There was no question: it was the ultimate promotion and an opportunity you didn't want to miss. The pulling (and selling) power of *Top of the Pops* meant that I had to pretty much drop everything and get to the studio asap. Bands and artists used to fly into London from all over the world to get their four minutes on that light-up stage in a dark corner of west London.

The only way my record company could get me back in time was by private plane. I got taken to the airport in a limousine. As we were waiting to board, the pilot came to speak to us. He said, 'If you want to go to the toilet, you need to go now because it's only a four-seater plane and there's no toilet on board.'

I laughed and said I'd better go, just in case.

When we boarded, he chuckled and said, 'I've just dropped off another very famous artist in Germany, and she got caught short. The only thing she could do was pee into the flask we usually use to serve hot drinks.'

Once we were airborne, he offered me a coffee. I thought, *No thanks, I know what that flask has been used for!*

My cousin Dorothy is a talented dressmaker, and she used to make a lot of my stage clothes for me. She made the outfit I wore on *Top of the Pops* for my 'It's a Heartache' performance, which was a royal-blue sequined three-piece suit with flared trousers, a waistcoat and a jacket. She also used to make the most gorgeous short dresses for me, and she would whip them up in a day if I asked her to. She was amazing – and she still is to this day. She used to have a shop back home where she sold clothes, some of them made by her and some bought by her in London. All the local girls used to snap them up!

I've never had a stylist, and I've always picked what I wanted to wear. I've never been told what to wear by anyone, aside from in the odd video when it fits in with the theme. I think you have to be comfortable with how you dress because if you're not, it shows.

I also found this great guy in Carnaby Street who used to make the most incredible suits. I'd go in and choose the fabric, and because he already had my measurements, sometimes they would be ready to collect later the same day. I used to wear loads of his suits on tour, and I wish he was still there now, because they were fabulous and cut especially for my body shape.

Even though I love clothes, packing has always been the bane of my career. Never knowing what to take and forgetting things . . . I hate packing, and I hate unpacking. That's the only thing I don't enjoy about travelling.

*

I was much more relaxed during that performance of *Top of the Pops*, as I think anyone watching it could tell. I still wasn't doing any proper dance moves, but I think I did a bit of swaying here and there.

I'm so grateful I'm not a nervous performer anymore. A long time has passed now, and the great thing about getting older is that you feel like you've got nothing to prove. You just get out there and enjoy yourself; it's second nature to me now. Some of my earlier success felt like it was overshadowed by stress and worry about how I looked and what I was going to wear – it took some of the enjoyment away. Everything was moving so fast, and I was always so nervous that I didn't get to enjoy what was happening as much as I should have done. Time was the only thing that changed the way I felt about myself. Now I'm not afraid to speak to anyone, and I strut around the stage like I own it!

*

I don't know what it was that made 'It's a Heartache' resonate with so many people, but maybe the new huskier tone in my voice was something to do with it? Perhaps my mother and I forgetting the strawberries and cream that day did me a favour! I don't think it was *hugely* different, because my voice had always been a bit husky, but it was sweeter before the operation. If you listen to 'Lost in France' and then 'It's a Heartache', you'll notice the difference. I feel lucky about that, because you do need something different about you to make it in the music industry – something that helps you stand out. You want people to hear a song and instantly think, *That's Bonnie Tyler!*

Having said that, I also believe in fate, and have done ever since I was young, so I don't think you have to have the best voice in the world if that path has already been planned out for you. When I was young, whenever we went somewhere with a wishing well, I would always throw in a penny and make a wish.

I still believe in wishes. I've got everything now that I could possibly want, but I do still ask for little things. I made a wish just a few weeks ago, and it came true. I pulled a wishbone with my husband, and I wished that I would be okay to sing at a show after being ill, and I was. I also wished that everyone would have a fantastic time, and I got a standing ovation and great reviews. Maybe that little wish helped me to bring it to life. I was so determined to make it an unforgettable night, and it was.

I wouldn't say I'm very superstitious overall, but pulling the wishbone after my mother had cooked a chicken was always something I did as a child to make my dreams come true.

For a long time, my dream was to marry Paul McCartney.

*

When I was a teenager, I remember having a huge poster of the Beatles above my bed that I'd torn out of an issue of *Jackie* magazine. It showed them in old-fashioned bathing suits and had autographs stamped on it, and because I was so young, I thought they were their real autographs. I was so proud of it, and I really treasured it.

I used to kiss Paul McCartney's signature every night because he was my favourite. I thought they were the business. Fast-forward fifteen years, and I finally got to meet him.

We were both recording in RAK Studios near Regent's Park. I'd been there for a couple of weeks, and I'd got to know the lovely receptionist quite well. When I walked past her one morning, she called me over and said in a hushed tone, 'Bonnie, you'll never believe who's in today. Paul McCartney!'

I was blown away. I replied, 'Oh my god, I would *love* to meet him!'

She told me to go into his studio and say hello, and assured me he wouldn't mind. I said I'd never have the nerve to do that!

The receptionist understood. She leaned forward and whispered, 'Make sure you make a lot of trips to the kitchen, in that case. He's always in there making tea!'

I thought there was no chance of spotting him, but I started making very frequent trips to get drinks just in case.

Sadly, there was no sign of him, and when I walked into the studio a few days later, the receptionist said to me, 'Bonnie, it's Paul's last day, so it's now or never. You need to knock on the door of the studio and chat to him!'

I thought, *Never in a million years would I interrupt one of the Beatles!* Anyway, she must have told Paul that I was dying to meet him but I didn't want to disturb him, because I was in my studio, standing by the piano practising some songs, and in walks Paul McCartney!

He sauntered over very coolly, just as you would expect Paul McCartney to do, and said, 'Hi, how are you doing? What are you up to?'

I was totally gaga. I couldn't believe it was really *him*, you know? I was so shocked I couldn't get any words out.

In the end, I managed to mumble something about going through some keys of songs. Then I said, 'Oh my god, I can't believe this. Wait until I tell my husband and mother that I've met you!' I was so nervous I told him about how I used to kiss his signature every night. Can you believe it? I said it in front of other people too!

He was so sweet about it and didn't make me feel at all embarrassed. Instead, he said, 'Let's have a kiss now,' and he leaned over and kissed me on the cheek. Well, I don't think I've ever turned as red as I did in that moment. He was such a gentleman.

As soon as he left, I got straight on the phone and rang my mother. I said to her, 'Oh Mammy, you'll never guess who just kissed me on the cheek.'

She replied, 'Oh, I don't care who it was. You'll never meet anybody as good as Robert.' She adored my husband so much. When I told her it was Paul McCartney, she said, 'I'm not bothered. No one is a match for your Robert.' It was so funny.

Shortly afterwards, Paul invited fifty people who were in the charts at the time, as well as some of the big DJs, for lunch at a vegetarian Chinese restaurant in west London. He was at number one with 'Mull of Kintyre' with his band Wings, and I was still at number four with 'It's a Heartache'. I remember Frankie Goes to Hollywood being there too, and I got to meet Linda McCartney, who was so lovely. The food was fantastic, and as I looked around the room, I couldn't quite believe I was there. It was like something out of a fantasy. How could I be having lunch with all these famous people? Me? I hadn't been around for very long, and there I was, surrounded by artists who had sold millions of records.

I met Paul again in Germany some years later, and I've got a photo where he is kissing me on the cheek again, and I'm making such a funny face – you would think it was a real hardship for me to get a kiss from my idol! I don't know if he was saying something to me and I was trying to answer, or if they caught me at a bad angle, but it's mortifying.

I have to say, even though I was in awe of all the amazing talent that was in the room at that lunch, I talked to the artists just like I would talk to anybody else. People often comment on the fact I don't act like I'm famous, but how else am I going to be? I appreciate everything that has happened for me, and I count my blessings. To me, one person is just like any other, whether they're famous or they work in a DIY store (unless it's Paul McCartney, of course!). We're all the same, at the end of the day, and I treat everyone equally.

I think growing up with such a big family and having no airs and graces kept me down to earth throughout everything. My family would never have let me get a big head, anyway. I may have been on *Top of the Pops*, but my parents acted like nothing had changed at all. I was just their Gaynor, and if we had family dinners, I had to help clear the plates from the table and wash up like everyone else. Quite right too.

I mean, look at my mother. If I went home after being away, she would still do my washing and ironing for me, just like she did when I was growing up. And if she came to stay with Robert and me, she loved getting into the kitchen and cooking. She always helped me out. People always used to stop her in the street and say, 'You must be so proud of your daughter.' And you know what she would say to them? 'Yes, I am, but I'm proud of *all* my children.' I think that's so lovely, and it's always stuck with me. And she was. She thought the world of all of us, no matter what we did. We were always good enough for her, and as long as we were happy, so was she.

*

'It's a Heartache' was continuing to sell well, and Ronnie thought there was no better time to try and secure a deal for me in America. He flew over to LA and had meetings with several record companies, but they all said the same thing: 'We like the song, but it's so hard to crack America.' No one wanted to take a (potentially very expensive) chance on me.

One of the record companies even had the cheek to ask Ronnie if he could record 'It's a Heartache' with Juice Newton and release it with her instead. She was already established in America, but Ronnie was so loyal he said no. Somehow, they did it anyway, and Ronnie Spector from The Ronettes also covered it and put it out. But it was *my* song!

This all went on at around the same time David suggested to Ronnie and Steve that, because I was getting so busy, they should bring in another manager who could look after me on a day-to-day basis so they had more time to produce and write songs. And before you could say 'What's New Pussycat?', Gordon Mills, who also managed Engelbert Humperdinck and Tom Jones, joined our little team.

By March, 'It's a Heartache' had also topped the charts in France, Australia, Canada, Norway and Sweden. And guess who came back wanting to sign me all of a sudden? Yep, the good old USA.

In the end, it was RCA in America who released the single, and their A&R manager Don Paulsen sent out a press release to radio stations that said: 'Dear reviewer, this is what the world thinks of "It's a Heartache" by Bonnie Tyler! Ordinarily, we don't send out singles. But this record, which RCA has rush-released in the US, is such an international smash that we wanted you to hear it.' Then he listed all the places it had already been a hit.

Both Ronnie and Juice's covers were released a few days before my version came out, but luckily for me, the radio stations only played my version. There are thousands of radio stations in America, and I was on nearly all of them. If you switched from one station to another, the chances are you would hear it.

The only fly in the ointment was that the most influential station in Los Angeles refused to play my song, because they only played tracks that had already made it into the top forty. That seemed ridiculous to me.

RCA found out that it was the main DJ's birthday, so they sent him a huge cake and told him to cut into it because he'd find a nice surprise. In the middle, where the jam should be, was a copy of 'It's a Heartache'. It was a great publicity stunt, and it bloody well worked! He thought the stunt was funny, so he asked for another copy – one that wasn't covered in cake – and he started playing the song. Soon the record was flying off the shelves, and it made it all the way to number three in the *Billboard* Hot 100.

I remember the record company saying they were sending me out to LA to do some promotion for the single. I asked them, 'Where's that?' They looked at me like I was mad and said, '*Los Angeles*?' It's fair to say I was still a bit naive at that point.

And so 'It's a Heartache' was the song that launched my career in America. I loved the song, but I didn't expect it to go as crazy as it did. I remember getting into a limo that was taking me from the airport to my hotel, and when I got in, the song was playing. I wanted to say to the driver, 'That's me, that is!' I was so excited, I wanted to wind the window down and shout out, 'This is my song!' to everyone we passed. Don't worry, I didn't . . .

I was put up at the swanky Beverley Hills Hotel. It had loads of palm trees and incredible-looking people wandering around. Even the people who worked there were stunning. It was like another world. I was staying in one of the bungalows in the grounds, and it was all decked out with antiques. It was surreal. This was my first time in America, and here I was, looking out the window at palm trees and a swimming pool, just a few miles away from the world-famous Hollywood sign.

Sadly, I wasn't there to have fun and get a tan. I was expected to work hard. I was up at 6am doing interviews over breakfast. I was jetlagged, and I'm not very good at getting up anyway, so I'm not sure the interviews made a lot of sense.

The hotel was so star-studded, one morning, I looked over and saw Neil Sedaka sitting at the next table, having coffee. As you do. After the interviews were finished, I'd visit lots of radio stations or meet up with record company executives, all the time hoping they would suddenly announce that they were going to give me a couple of hours off to go shopping on Rodeo Drive. If only!

One evening, while we were chatting about work, Gordon asked if I wanted to open for Tom Jones when he did some shows later that week. I didn't need to be asked twice. My schedule was *crazy*, but how could I turn down an opportunity like that? Tom flipping Jones!

Within a few days, I found myself on stage at the Greek Theatre, one of LA's coolest gig venues. It was total madness, but also very buzzy and exciting. I supported Tom for five nights in all, and each one felt better than the last. He is wonderful. His voice is so incredible – one of those you could never mistake for anyone else – and it's still going strong.

I'm not sure I've ever been as nervous as I was that first night. Off stage, I was still Gaynor from the village, and then I had to go on stage and have a different persona. No one wants to watch a nervous girl singing a song – they want a bit of an atmosphere. I did my best, but I was opening for Tom Jones, who has the most incredible stage presence. It was very intimidating.

I had performed with Bobby Wayne as a Dixie for so long, and then after that, I was always with Imagination, so I was used to having people backing me up and not all the attention being focused on me. For those shows, I pretty much stayed in one spot and sang. I could get away with it back then, because songs like 'Lost in France' and 'It's a Heartache' suited that kind of performance. Being rooted to the spot due to nerves wasn't how I wanted to spend my career, though, so I had to step (no pun intended) outside of my comfort zone and start being braver. I started to enjoy using the stage a bit more. These days, there's no stopping me. I'm always running from one side of the stage to the other and getting the audience to sing along. The rockier songs that came later helped with that – they gave me fire and freedom. They're great stage material.

I think as you get older, you feel like you've got nothing to prove, and that's a great way to be. Now I feel so at home on stage, it seems strange to think I was ever any different.

*

It was an incredible experience supporting Tom. I'd watch him from the side of the stage, and after the shows, we'd all go out for dinner, and there would be about thirteen of us eating and drinking and chatting. I was so shy I was never the one in the middle of the conversations, even after a few drinks. I'd sit back and listen to everyone talk about all these amazing things they had done. They were wonderful times that are great to look back on. Tom was always great and friendly, but I was far too nervous to strike up a conversation with him, so we didn't talk a lot. But he did sign an autograph for me, writing 'Cymru am byth!' ('Wales forever!') by it. We both did the same charity concert for the Royal Marsden Hospital in London in 2020, but because of Covid, we weren't able to chat much then either because we had to keep our distance. I wouldn't be able to brag and say he's a friend of mine – and I don't have his number or anything like that – but from what I know about him, he's a lovely man.

After I finished supporting Tom, I went out on my own mini-tour to Dallas, Nashville, Atlanta, Chicago and New York. Carole King came to see me perform in LA, Willie Nelson came to see me in Nashville and Emmylou Harris was in the audience in New York. Talk about flattering! I was also presented with a platinum disc in New York for selling over 100,000 albums in Canada, so all in all, it was an unbelievable couple of weeks. What a great experience for a girl from Skewen.

Imagination came with me on the US tour, and it was lovely to have people I knew by my side. They also toured with me in the UK and Europe. It was a huge expense for the record company, because the band were having to travel from Wales to London and stay in hotels so they could be at the airport the following day.

After a while, RCA said it was costing too much, and so Ronnie and Steve put a band together who were based in London and said I had to tour with them going forward. I was gutted because I was really good friends with Imagination, and we'd been through a lot together.

As far as I know, Imagination carried on working as musicians back in Wales. I know for certain that Kevin did, because our paths crossed much later on in a way I really wasn't expecting – but we'll come to that in a bit.

The band I have now have been with me for nearly thirty years, apart from the drummer, Alex Toff, who joined seven years ago. We travel and tour all over the world together, but they do all sorts of other things when they're not performing with me. My lead guitarist, Matt Prior, is also a great producer, and does a lot of music for Formula One. My drummer also works with Belinda Carlisle, and my bass player, Ed Poole, used to be in a band called Romeo's Daughter. He also performs with other artists. When my keyboard player, John

Young, isn't working with me, he's got his own band called Lifesigns, who recently toured Europe.

They're a great, fun group of guys. They're very generous, and they do their very best to be available to tour with me, but I appreciate that sometimes they have other things going on. We've been together for such a long time that it all feels very natural and easy. If you're going to spend that much time together, you have to feel relaxed and comfortable around each other.

*

I was still quite unsure of myself during that first tour in America, and I didn't feel like a pop star or as if I was famous in any way, even though I'd had two big hits and was becoming better known over there as the weeks went by.

There wasn't a time when it suddenly hit me that I was successful, because I still felt like me. I know a lot of people change when they get a taste of fame, but I was never going to be that person who went to wild parties and woke up not knowing what she had done the night before. I liked going out for dinner with people I worked with and having nice conversations. Some people may think that was a missed opportunity, because I could have been living the high life every night and going to fancy parties in the Hollywood Hills, but I couldn't think of anything worse.

I did go out sometimes, of course, because I was invited to work events and parties where I had to go along and meet a certain person or show my face. But I always, always wanted to be professional, so I would do my best to make sure I got enough sleep and was always on time and ready to do what was asked of me.

I guess you could say I lived a bit of a dual life back in the early days. Half of my life involved being at home in Wales, having a cup of tea with my mother or dinner with Robert, while the other half was living this life where I'd get put up in amazing hotels and do shows with Tom Jones.

To be honest, I always felt like I didn't do enough promotion in America around that time. I feel like I should have stayed there for longer and established myself, and that is a bit of a regret I have. I don't like to regret things, but I do think I missed an opportunity to do more because I was feeling homesick. I found it so hard being away from everyone I loved, and I couldn't wait to be back in Wales.

I missed Robert like crazy when I was travelling, but after about three years of me having more hit records, we realised that it could last a lot longer than we thought. I was still with RCA, and even though I was nearing the end of my five-year contract, my management were keen to carry on making music with me. They said I wouldn't have a problem getting another deal, so why stop?

In the end, I said to Robert, 'You know, I have been so lucky to have all these hit records and travel to so many different places, but it's not the same if you're not with me. I don't want to do it anymore if you're not by my side. Unless you want to travel with me, I'm not going to sign another record deal. I'll gladly give it up and come back to Wales and do residencies in local clubs again.'

I would have been very happy to do that. The fame side of things never meant much to me. I loved singing, and I didn't mind where I did it: on stage in front of thousands of people, on a TV show watched by millions, or in a club with a couple of hundred people dancing and having fun. Nothing was tying me to my career. It was all about singing, and I could do that anywhere. I will admit the money was good, but we had saved up quite a bit, and Robert was a hard worker, so between us, we had enough to live a nice life if we both carried on working in the same clubs as we had done for so long.

We had a long discussion about it, and in the end, Robert told me he didn't want me to turn my back on my career and miss any opportunities that may lie ahead. He knew how much I missed him, and he also missed me, so it proved to be a big turning point for us. My career didn't harm our relationship because we were so in love, but being so in love made it even harder every time I had to go away and leave him.

We decided that Robert was going to start travelling everywhere with me, and it made something that was already fun and exciting even more fun and exciting. I had my best friend and the love of my life there to enjoy all the special moments with me. Who wouldn't want that? I always joke that he's my biggest fan because he's seen so many of my shows, but it's not like he's had much of a choice!

Fame can be a funny thing to navigate, and it can get lonely. You hear stories about people who perform to 10,000 people, and then they go back to their hotel room, and they're alone. It's no wonder they tuck into the mini bar or get room service, because you go from this massive high to a massive low.

I think because I always travelled with other people, I was never in any danger of being put in difficult situations or having anything bad happen to me. The #MeToo movement has been huge over the past few years, but I didn't ever get caught up in anything like that. I didn't see myself as someone men would want to hit on anyway, and I always felt very well looked after and protected. People joked that once Robert started travelling with me, he was like my bodyguard because of his judo prowess. I know he would have come in handy if anything had happened, but I'd never felt the need for a bodyguard. Maybe they were different times, but I always felt safe.

It's wonderful that Robert and I have travelled the world together over and over, and we still do now. Looking back, that was when I first really started to enjoy all the country-hopping.

Don't get me wrong, I was always very grateful for it, and my band and my managers were great friends of mine. But having Robert with me changed things, and it was like I was seeing each place for the first time because he was. We would go out exploring together and visit new places all the time. I did things I probably would never have done on my own. It also made being in hotels a nicer experience. In the beginning, it felt like a treat to stay in hotels, but after a few years, they all started to look the same and all I wanted was my own bed. Being with Robert took that feeling away. I still missed my friends and my family a lot, but I always had that reminder of home in my husband.

*

My second album, *Natural Force*, came out in the UK in May 1978. My band, Robert and I went on tour around the UK and Europe, and we had a bloody great time. Meanwhile, in the US, the album went to number sixteen on the *Billboard* chart and reached number two on the Top Country Albums chart. It seemed I was, as they say, Big in America.

I was being invited on to shows, left, right and centre – and was even invited to perform on *The Kenny Everett Video Show*! I was also invited on to *The David Frost Show* in 1978, appearing alongside Muhammad Ali and James Stewart. I was desperate to ask Muhammad for his autograph for my father, because he was such a huge fan, but I was nervous because I imagined he got asked every single day of his life. I also thought it might be a bit odd to ask someone for their autograph when you've just been sitting next to them on a chat show. The funny thing is that before I got a chance to ask him for his, he asked me for *mine.* It turned out a member of his family was a fan! I was chuffed to bits, and when I asked him for his, he was more than happy to do it. He didn't mind at all. He was a real gentleman. Later on in my career I was so thrilled to meet up with him again, and I ended up getting another autograph from him.

My father was so proud that I'd met Muhammad Ali. Obviously, he'd been a boxer too, only on a slightly smaller scale! When I gave him the autograph, he showed it to everyone. And I mean *everyone.* I don't think there was a single person in our village who didn't know that my father had Muhammad Ali's autograph in his wallet.

I found that autograph after my father passed away, so I've got them both now. One of them is ripped, but you can still tell what it is. I bet they're worth a fortune, but I'd never sell them. They're two of my treasures, especially as one of them belonged to my father.

I met Muhammad Ali again when I was invited to Radio

City to sing 'Holding Out for a Hero' in the nineties. They were hosting an event called 'Night of 100 Stars', and they asked me to fly to New York to be in the finale of the show. I'd just cut my hair into a bob, and it looked awful. No one had even heard of hair extensions in the nineties, so I was stuck with it – and I hated it.

Hair aside, it was the most fabulous night. I was asked to slide down a fireman's pole and then launch into the song, and I was totally up for it. I could do that kind of thing back then!

After I had performed, I had to welcome all these stars on to the stage, including Marilyn Monroe's ex-husband Joe DiMaggio, Joe Frasier and Muhammad Ali. By that time, Muhammad was very unwell due to having Parkinson's disease. He was very slow walking on to the stage, but it was so lovely to see him. I don't know if I was starstruck, but I was very nervous introducing everybody. I was told to kiss all the men on the cheek, so I got kisses from lots of lovely famous gentlemen!

There was a drinks party afterwards at the Tiffany store – the one from the Audrey Hepburn film! – and everyone who was anyone was there. I turned around and came face to face with Raquel Welch, and I was taken aback by how beautiful she was in real life. She was even more stunning in person than she was onscreen.

I must admit, I've had a couple of little blue boxes myself over the years, and I cherish them. There's something very special about them.

CHAPTER FOUR

Total Eclipse of the Charts

Towards the end of the seventies, Steve, Ronnie and David had a professional disagreement over a song that Ronnie and Steve had written and wanted to release as a follow-up to 'It's a Heartache'. David thought it was a good song but not good *enough*, as he didn't see it being a hit. Ronnie was determined it should be my next release, and persuaded David to redo the production with them sitting by and approving each step of the way. When it was completed, Ronnie was happy, but David still said, 'I don't honestly think it's a hit.' Steve was stuck in the middle but, being a part-manager, he sided with Ronnie. Ronnie told David he was convinced it was a hit and that he would find another producer to take over my recording. And that was the end of their working relationship. They brought in a new producer called Robin Geoffrey Cable.

David and I didn't fall out, but didn't see each other for years after that. It hit me hard because David was such a lovely man and I knew he only wanted what was best for me, but as Steve and Ronnie were still my managers, I couldn't take sides and I had no choice but to stay with them.

I released an album in 1979 called *Diamond Cut* that I wasn't very happy with. It contained a song by Tom Petty called 'Louisiana Rain', which some of you will know was a big hit for him when he released it the following year. My managers and the record company wanted to take me down this country road that I just wasn't comfortable with. I'd had success in the country charts, and they wanted to capitalise on that. They wanted to make me a British country star to rival Crystal Gayle, singing tracks about loneliness and heartbreak. It was so sentimental. I wanted to be wearing leather trousers and belting out bangers!

Robin was an amazing producer who had worked on huge hits like Chris de Burgh's 'A Spaceman Came Travelling' and Carly Simon's 'You're So Vain', but I didn't want to spend the rest of my career sitting on a stool singing about break-ups. An American journalist who wrote a review of my album said: 'I cannot help but wonder if the people behind Bonnie Tyler realise just what they have on their hands. In her pictures, she looks like this sweet little country girl . . . but, I swear, when she opens her mouth to sing, out comes the voice of Janis Joplin.' At least someone was seeing – or rather hearing – the 'me' that was bursting to come out!

The only positive things were that I had a big hit in France with the song 'My Guns Are Loaded'. Apart from that, the album didn't do an awful lot. It's hard to promote something you don't believe in.

I went in a different direction when I was asked to sing on the soundtrack to the film adaptation of the Jackie Collins novel *The World is Full of Married Men*, which came out that year. It had more of a disco sound, so that was a different genre again, but still not one that suited my voice that well. It was a minor hit in the UK, getting to number thirty-four, and if you wait right until the end of the movie, you'll see me appear on screen singing as the credits are rolling. That was my first – and my last – movie appearance.

Steve and Ronnie decided to take me to Japan to gauge interest. The Japanese market is notoriously lucrative, and they had spotted an opportunity after seeing an advert for the Yamaha World Popular Song Festival, which was being held at the Nippon Budokan Hall in Tokyo.

The poster read: 'Songwriters! Singers! Your best is all you need to come celebrate our 10th anniversary with us. You'll need a demo tape, music score and lyrics, bio and photo, and a completed application form. Entry deadline 10 July 1979.'

We filled out the form, and off we went.

I wore a very shiny trouser suit and represented the UK singing a song called 'Sitting on the Edge of the Ocean', which Ronnie and Steve had written. Sixteen countries entered. When I got down to the final eight, I was amazed. When they read out the final results, I didn't think for a minute I was going to win, but I bloody did! I jumped out of my seat, and I remember a million flashbulbs going off. I was stunned, because I was competing against Cissy Houston, who had the most incredible voice. She came second, but I was convinced she would be going home with the trophy. Instead, I won the Grand Prix award, which equalled a certificate, a gold medal and $5,000 cash.

I met Cissy's daughter Whitney that day. She was only sixteen and was yet to start her incredible career. She was so pretty and angelic, and she was wearing these big reading glasses. She came over to me slightly nervously and said, 'Bonnie, can I have your autograph, please?' I had no idea she was going to go on to become a world-famous megastar. Our paths never crossed again, but I think she was one of the most talented female singers who ever lived. What a voice she had.

*

'Sitting on the Edge of the Ocean' was one of the tracks that featured on my fourth album, 1981's *Goodbye to the Island*. I also did a cover of Procol Harum's 'A Whiter Shade of Pale' for that album, as I love that song. People always went crazy when I know it's one of those songs that people think you should never cover because how can you improve on the original? But I know it means a lot to many people. That summer of 1967 felt more carefree somehow, and as if everyone was united. It was daring, I'll give you that. That was when I used to go to the Top Rank with my friend Christine or my cousin Christine on Tuesdays and Thursdays, and sometimes Saturdays too. It's when I got interested in boys for the first time as well, I suppose. I was a useless dancer, but I still really enjoyed it.

If I stayed at my cousin Christine's, we used to let ourselves in using a key that was hanging down on a piece of string, arriving home a lot later than we were told to. More often than not Auntie Kate would hear us creeping up the stairs and shout the house down! Christine and I used to go to her room and laugh about being told off again. It was such a fun time.

I recorded most of *Goodbye to the Island* in a mobile studio in Portugal in the summer of 1980, and that's when Robert and I fell in love with the place. I worked every bit as hard as I always do, but it was different because it was sunny and beautiful, which meant everyone was in a good mood all the time. It made a nice difference from rainy London, but the downside was that when I was in the studio, I wanted to keep popping out for some fresh air and a hit of Mediterranean sun. I needed that breeze after being in a hot studio for several hours.

I thought Portugal was so beautiful. Ronnie had decided he was going to buy a place over there, and he was looking around Vilamoura because there was a really good school close by that he wanted his daughter, Louisa, to go to. He knew we were interested in looking for a house there, so he asked Robert and me if we would go and look at two villas with him and his wife, Joan, because they couldn't decide between the two. We looked at the first one, and it was very nice, but it didn't knock my socks off. When we went to see the second, I walked in, looked at the view of the sea and said, 'This is it, this is the one! But *I* want it!' I had my fingers crossed that it wouldn't be suitable for Ronnie because it was too far away from the school they'd chosen.

It turned out the place wasn't right for him, but I had fallen head over heels for it, and we started thinking about buying a place in Portugal too. We went and looked at some other properties, but I kept being drawn back to that villa. It felt right, so we *did* buy it – and we couldn't have picked better. We've had it for so long now that we've had it knocked down and rebuilt over the years. Our house in Wales is beautiful and old, built in 1850, but our villa is ultra-modern, and it's nice to have both. I feel cosy at home in Wales and so free and happy in Portugal. To me, Portugal is like paradise. I'm never happier than when I'm relaxing there with Robert, and we've got so many lovely friends out there.

We've got a lovely piano in our house in Wales, and I did try and learn to play once, because I thought it would be great if I could play on stage. But while I was okay with the theory side of learning, I couldn't play the damn thing, so that went out the window (not the actual piano!).

I have to say, buying our villa was probably the best thing about recording that album. That time in Portugal wasn't a holiday in any way. I didn't come back with a hangover and an amazing tan, just an album I felt disappointed by.

My heart wasn't in it anymore, and I wasn't enjoying the singing process because I didn't like the music. I started to feel a bit like a puppet. Steve and Ronnie were very nice guys and our relationship was fine, but they couldn't see further than me singing middle-of-the-road country tracks.

After five years with RCA, I knew I was ready to leave.

*

I'd come straight to RCA from the clubs in Wales, and I had been doing what I was told was right. It's really hard to stop a train when other people are driving it. In the early days, my records had been hits all around the world, and that meant I'd had such a packed schedule of promotional appearances, performances, record signings and TV shows that I didn't stop and wonder if I was truly happy.

But now I was beginning to ask myself that question.

The problem was, my music was doing well. I already had twelve gold discs, and I'd won several awards. Because 'It's a Heartache' had been a hit on the American country charts, they were still hoping that, at some point, I would crack the American country market. All of this meant that no record company exec was going to step in and say, 'Let's take a risk and change the sound!' But I was desperate to. I wanted to go more rock, and they weren't open to that at all. I disliked my last two albums so much I didn't even play them (not that I sit at home listening to my own albums all the time!).

I did, and still do, love country music, but I felt like my sound was a bit washed out and safe. I thought to myself, *I only get one career, and I want to make the most of it. I want to perform the kind of songs that make me feel alive.*

RCA wanted to re-sign me for another five years, but I said, 'No. I want to move on and do rockier songs.'

And that was that.

It also meant I had to walk away from Steve Wolfe and Ronnie Scott, which was an incredibly hard thing to do. Even though it was 100 per cent the right thing, I felt disloyal, like I was letting them down. They had built up my career and backed me all the way. They had worked hard for me, and in return, I had worked bloody hard for them. But the rapport and the excitement that had been there during our first few years of working together had withered away. I still respected them a lot, but I didn't think we were the right fit for each other anymore.

It was a tough moment when I said to them both, 'Please don't take it personally, but I want to do different things.'

Ronnie replied, 'I think you're wrong, darling, but you have to do what you want to do.'

That's how well we got on. It was so kind of him. That conversation could have gone very differently. They would have been well within their rights to be angry; after all, they had discovered me and given me the most amazing opportunities. But did that mean I owed them the rest of my career? Should I have stayed with them out of guilt? I think they would have hated that as much as I would have done. They were very gracious, and there was no bad blood, although they were probably thinking, *Bonnie, a rock star? Well, this is going to be interesting to watch!*

Ronnie and Steve were always upfront and honest with me. I've been lucky that I've never been ripped off during my career, and they were the ones who taught me everything I needed to know. They treated me with a lot of respect, and I knew I would miss them a lot.

*

It was a massive risk turning my back on career security. I had wanted success, and hadn't I achieved it? I'd been on *Top of the Pops*, had some great hits and released four albums. On the flip side, *Diamond Cut* and *Goodbye to the Island* weren't what you'd call massive hits, and it had been a while since I'd had a big hit single, so the offers to perform shows dried up a lot, and that was the bit I enjoyed. I had veered so far away from the music I loved, and I think people could probably tell that, now the initial excitement of being a pop star had worn off, the passion just wasn't there. People aren't stupid.

I was determined I wasn't going to be someone who only had a few good years. But you don't often get a second chance in the music industry. Once you're out, it's very hard to tunnel your way back in, and I knew I had so much more inside me. I didn't want to be a throwaway singer.

My head was a mess. I spent several months wondering if I'd done the right thing, but I had to cling to the hope that I would find an authentic sound and make an album I was proud of. I had to white-knuckle it, but not for one minute did I regret saying no to RCA. I just had to hold my nerve. I said to Robert that I would give things one more shot, and if I couldn't go in a different direction and get another music deal, I would go back to singing in the clubs. You can bet your life I would still have been working and singing in some capacity, whether I had chart success again or not. I didn't want to be a star; I wanted to be a singer. I had been fortunate that I had been discovered and got a record deal, but I didn't go searching for it – I didn't ever send tapes of myself singing to record companies, or anything like that. So if I went back to being a resident singer in the local clubs, it really wouldn't have fazed me.

I started listening again to the kind of music I loved and records that made me feel alive. Even though I had wavered off the road to hit records and found myself in a musical cul-de-sac, I still believed in myself. I had to. No one else was going to do this for me.

I threw myself into listening to tapes of demos to find songs that I loved, and that would also suit my voice. I listened to about 500 cassettes in all, which my new manager, David Aspden, had sent me via different publishers.

I met David when he worked as a TV plugger at RCA. He used to organise TV appearances for all the RCA artists, including David Bowie, and he had also worked with Ronnie and Steve. He'd always thought I should be doing rockier stuff. When there were discussions with RCA about me trying to make some grittier songs, he always supported me. I knew David had a similar vision, so I asked him if he would manage me. He thought about it for a couple of weeks, and then he agreed, so he left RCA and took over managing me full-time.

He was much more proactive and, I guess, more serious than Ronnie and Steve. He had worked in a record company for a long time, and they can be very cut-throat. You need someone who's prepared to go into battle for you, and I felt like David was that man.

Over the next few months, I whittled those 500 songs down to the twenty I felt best represented me. David and I made demos of them all, and from those twenty, we chose the five we thought were the strongest. Once we had finished that process, which took almost two years in total, David sent the demos to a record label called CBS. He knew they had a strong roster of rock musicians, and I wanted to be their latest signing. And, believe it or not, I was! After a meeting with some of the big execs, I was offered a five-year deal.

My white-knuckling had paid off; now all I had to do was put my plan for rock world domination into action. At the very least, I'd give it a bloody good go.

I had my first big meeting with Muff Winwood, the head of A&R at CBS (two great facts about Muff: he used to be in the Spencer Davis Group and he is singer Steve Winwood's brother). He said to me, 'Right Bonnie, what direction would you like to go in?'

I replied, 'I would love to work with whoever it is that writes and produces Meat Loaf.'

He looked like someone had just told him aliens had landed on the roof of the record company. He clearly thought I was

Before Bonnie, I was Gaynor Hopkins from Skewen (pictured here at school, aged 9).

On holiday at Happy Valley in Porthcawl. Left to right: Mammy, my sister Avis's husband Billy, Mam Hopkins, Daddy, niece Shireen and Avis.

The Three Musketeers: Uncle Frank, Dad and Uncle Ernie in uniform. Weren't they so handsome!

One of the earliest photos I can remember – me (with a dummy and a doll under my arm), my mother and my sister Angela.

Me (in the hat) with my little sister Avis and our mother.

Aged 14 and posing in our garden at Cwrt-Y-Clafdy, with my little brother Paul's toy tractors in the background.

My schoolfriend Diane and me, back when Miners pale pink lipstick was in fashion. Her parents would drive us to all sorts of places on the weekends in their Morris 1000.

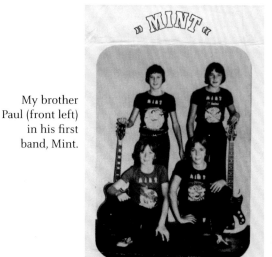

My brother Paul (front left) in his first band, Mint.

Talent scout Roger Bell, who discovered me when I was performing at the Townsman, pictured here with his wife Vura and daughter Denni.

Bobby Wayne and the Dixies. Left: Bobby Wayne (standing), Rita Marvin and Peter James. Right: Toni Carol, me and Ronnie Williams.

Robert (second from right) and the judo team who represented Great Britain at the 1972 Olympic Games in Munich.

Robert and me on our wedding day in 1973. I couldn't have wished for a more perfect day (even if my hair was maybe a little too blonde and curly!)

My wonderful siblings and their lovely spouses. L-R: (back) Lynn, Teresa, Margaret, Angela, Avis, Gwyn and Marlene; (front) me, Robert and Jan.

My little brother Paul was gigging that night and couldn't be in the photo – so here he is!

(Left) Imagination, the band I joined after my time in the Dixies. L–R: Me (as Shereen), Robert Grinter, Kevin Dunne and Mike Adams. We played all kinds of music all over the place.

(Right) My first tour of the USA with (L–R) Toni Lambert, Steve Laurie, Neil Adams, Kevin Dunne and Gary Hayman.

Robert looking dashing in his judo kit. The local paper captioned this with 'The girl Bobby fell for'!

World-famous producer and songwriter Jim Steinman, who I worked with on 'Total Eclipse of the Heart'.

Me and my beloved father, Glyn.

My mother, Elsie, singing by my grand piano. She had the most beautiful voice but was so shy!

Robert and me on a skiing holiday. We still love to travel the world together.

The two of us on board our yacht, *Angel*. I loved that boat!

My parents relaxing at our house in Portugal.

My brother Paul's boys, Andrew and James. I have sixteen (sixteen!) nieces and nephews, and I love them all.

Belting out the hits
at the Montreux Rock
Festival in peak 'Total
Eclipse' era – big hair,
even bigger voice!

A peck on the cheek
from my teenage
crush, Paul McCartney,
at a fundraiser concert
we both performed at
in Germany.

Little Steven, me and Jon Bon Jovi backstage at the Madison Square Garden, New York.

A massive career highlight: performing for and meeting Pope Francis in 2019.

Terry Wogan first had me on his show in 1983, alongside none other than Tina Turner. Two one-of-a-kinds who are dearly missed.

Catherine Zeta-Jones is my husband's second cousin – I was so happy to be at her beautiful wedding to Michael Douglas in 2000.

My awesome band, L–R: Alex Toff, Ed Poole, me, John Young and Matt Prior.

I met Whitney Houston when she was just a teenager, before her career took off. And to think that she asked for my autograph!

Robert and me on a sightseeing tour in Greenland with my band and crew.

Me with Sir Alex Ferguson at the Grand National in 2013. I can talk to anybody (even if I know next to nothing about football . . .)

Representing the UK in the 2013 Eurovision Song Contest in Malmö, Sweden – forty years after I'd first been asked!

A real 'pinch me' moment: being awarded my MBE by the Prince of Wales in February 2023. What would little Gaynor Hopkins from Skewen have thought?

mad. He laughed and said, 'Are you crazy? That's *Jim Steinman!*' I said, 'I love the *Bat Out of Hell* album, the music and the production, and I know I can do that sort of powerful, majestic, in-your-face pop rock.'

Muff said there was no way Jim would work with me when I had been out of the industry for so long and had been known for being a country-pop star, but I pleaded my case and asked him to at least make some enquiries. I mean, if you don't ask, you never know, do you? He shrugged his shoulders and agreed to put out some feelers, but warned me to prepare myself for bad news.

Muff came back to me a few days later and said that Jim was very confused and didn't understand why I wanted to work with him. He knew who I was, because 'It's a Heartache' had been such a big hit over there, but it was a million miles away from the style of music Jim did. He didn't understand why Bonnie Tyler, of all people, wanted to get into the studio with him. He effectively said thanks but no thanks, and I was gutted.

As I was mulling over plan Bs, none of which came close to the idea of working with Jim, I was thrown a lifeline. Jim had thought things over and asked CBS in America to send him some of my demos. I had to wait three agonising weeks for him to get back to the record company, and then word reached me that he had made a decision. He wanted to meet me.

My first thought was, *This is fucking brilliant!* And my second thought was, *This is fucking brilliant!*

Apparently, after mulling it over for a while, Jim had found my request to work with him so bizarre and interesting, he didn't feel like he could say a firm no without giving me a chance first. He was also intrigued that we had a shared interest in Phil Spector's 'Wall of Sound' technique. I thought Tina Turner's 'River Deep – Mountain High' had some of the best production I'd ever heard, and Jim was a big fan too.

Jim told my record company that he felt like I had 'an eighties voice that hadn't been exploited', or something along those lines. I didn't care what he said about me, as long as he agreed to work with me.

David and I flew to New York to meet Jim Steinman a few weeks later. He lived in this huge, splendid apartment overlooking Central Park. His next-door neighbour was Dustin Hoffman. I mean, talk about glamorous. It wasn't the sort of place where you could just walk in and get into the lift. We had to be checked in by the doormen, and then they rang Jim to let him know we were there. I was finally going to meet the maestro, and I was so excited and nervous!

We got into the lift and went straight to the top floor, where the penthouse apartments were. When we stepped out of the lift, there was a line of sweets leading to a door. The film *E.T.* was out at the time, and E.T. does something similar. Jim had laid out this line of M&M's so we knew which apartment to go to. I tell you, I was not expecting that!

The door to the apartment was massive, with an oval pane of frosted glass in it. We rang the doorbell, and Jim opened the door. He had this wild, flowing hair covering his face, and I thought to myself, *He looks like someone out of the Addams family!* He invited us straight through into his kitchen, which was stacked with cassette tapes. There were no CDs in the eighties, so there were tapes everywhere you looked. There's no way you could have eaten dinner at the table because it was piled high with all these cassettes.

Jim's apartment was incredible. He showed us into the sitting room, where he had crystal pyramids and weird gothic art everywhere, as well as a beautiful grand piano. He offered us some drinks, and then he said to me, 'I'll play you some songs, and you can see what you think.'

Jim was a wine fanatic and had special fridges to keep them all at the right temperature. Loads of them! There were several bottles open on the table with about three inches left in the bottom of them all. He only drank very, *very* expensive wine – but he never drank the last glass in every bottle.

I felt comfortable with him straight away, and it was one of those moments that makes you take stock of your life. David and I were standing in Jim Steinman's apartment looking out on to Central Park. It was what I'd wished for, and now, as if by magic, here I was. How I ever thought he'd want to work with me, I don't know, but it was like there was a voice inside me telling me I *had* to at least try.

Jim played us some great new songs we hadn't heard before, and then he played me Blue Oyster Cult's 'Goin' Through The Motions' and a couple of Creedence Clearwater tracks, including 'Have You Ever Seen the Rain?' He asked me what I thought of them.

David and I loved them all, and we told him so. Jim later admitted to a DJ called Tony Prince that if I hadn't liked them, it would have been a very short meeting. Thank goodness I didn't say they were rubbish, because he wouldn't have even entertained the idea of working with me if we hadn't been on the same page.

He asked if I wanted to do covers of both songs and I instantly said yes. Bear in mind I was still very shy, even at that point in my career. I only really had confidence when I was on stage. But that day kind of sealed the deal, and we agreed that I would go ahead and do the covers and he would work with me on them.

We flew back to London on such a high, not believing what had just happened. Not only had I somehow managed to meet Jim, but we were also going to work together. Oh. My. God. I had bloody done it.

That was the beginning of my working with Jim after so many people laughed and told me it would never happen. I just *knew* it would. I have good instincts, and I listen to them, and I follow through. I always go with my gut feeling. On the very rare occasions I've gone against my instincts, I've always regretted it. That's one of the reasons I stick to my guns.

The news that Bonnie Tyler and Jim Steinman were teaming up was a shock to a lot of people. I remember the pop magazine called *Smash Hits* writing a piece where they wrote about how astonished they were that Jim had agreed to work with me. How rude!

Three weeks later, Jim called David and me back to New York because he had a song he wanted to play for me. I didn't know what to expect, because Jim never gave artists tapes of songs in advance; he always wanted you to make the song your own rather than mimicking a demo. You didn't get a huge amount of direction, but that's what made it all so exciting. It was the exact opposite of singing by numbers. You had to dig deep and find what worked best for the song.

We went to David Sonenberg's (Jim's manager's) office, a very plush place. The Canadian singer Rory Dodd was also there when we arrived. Jim told us about this song that he had started writing many, many years before, but had never finished. That song was 'Total Eclipse of the Heart'. He had originally composed it for a musical called *Dance of the Vampires*.

Rory started singing the song while Jim played the music on the grand piano with such passion I thought it was going to fall through the floor. David and I just looked at each other, each of us thinking, 'Wow! This is bloody *amazing*!'

When they finished performing, Jim said he was going to give me the song to record.

And I just knew.

I knew this was the song I had been waiting for all my life.

*

'Total Eclipse' was flawless – apart from one thing. Because Jim had started writing it for a musical, it was over seven minutes long. Imagine trying to get that on *Top of the Pops*. It would take up half of the show! Jim was heartbroken when it had to be cut down to four minutes and thirty seconds so it could get some radio play.

Meat Loaf was also gutted that Jim didn't give him that song, and apparently, he phoned him up to ask him why he'd given it to me instead. Whenever I saw Meat Loaf, he used to say to me, 'That song was mine!' To this day, I have no idea why Jim chose me to record it, but I'm so glad he did. I am forever grateful because it's an evergreen song that will be played for so many years to come.

I knew when we were recording 'Total Eclipse' that there was something magical about it. I was so excited about releasing it – but first, we had to film the video.

We filmed it at the Holloway Sanatorium, which is this huge gothic Victorian hospital near Virginia Water in Surrey. I'll tell you what, it's a bloody scary place. It's guarded by six security guards and six dogs. Do you know how they say dogs can sense things? Well, the security guards told us that the dogs wouldn't go anywhere near what used to be the morgue, and they also won't set foot (paw?) in the room where doctors used to administer electric shocks to patients. It was a genuinely terrifying building, but it did suit the tone of the song.

Jim Steinman wrote the storyboard and directed the video, and he added in all sorts of crazy things like American footballers and doves. Of course he did – his mind was amazing! It was also amazing that he got me to wear a dress. It's one of the few times I have, but it was a gorgeous one, mind.

There was a famous film director on the production team who I don't think liked me very much because I kept asking questions. I was asked to do some strange things, and every time I said, 'Do I really have to do this?' or 'Why are we doing that?', he kept rolling his eyes. I found the video very confusing. I think people still do now. I was supposed to be dreaming the entire video, which is why some of it makes absolutely no sense, because I guess dreams make no sense? They skip from one thing to another, which is why you can never remember the bloody things properly.

My goodness, though, that video was hard work. It was relentless. We started at 9.30am in the middle of winter, so it was freezing cold and finished at 3.30am the following day, shortly after I'd been chased barefoot through the snow by pagan dancers.

At one point, there's a young chap sitting in a chair, and he releases a dove. At first, they wanted to shoot the scene so he was naked. I said, 'You've got absolutely no chance; he's a little boy.' They put him in a school uniform in the end.

Two of the boys in the main dinner party scene ended up in hospital. When they had to do the fight scene, they flipped over the table, and a glass dish broke. These poor boys fell on it and cut themselves, and they had to go off and get stitched up.

Even though I was exhausted at the end of filming, it all turned out to be worth it. It was on heavy rotation on an exciting new channel called MTV, which had just started up. That channel was a gift for the song. I went to the MTV studios in downtown New York many times to do interviews. Even now, whenever I do TV shows, they play a clip of that video, and it's had almost a billion views on YouTube.

There have been some great parodies of the video over the years. There's the 'literal' version that loads of people will have seen or heard of. It's my video and soundtrack, but with someone singing different lyrics over the top describing what's going on in the video. It's so funny. If you haven't seen it, have a look at it on YouTube.

My favourite one, though, is a Lego version of the video.

My head falls off in one bit! People always ask me what I think of the parodies, as if I'm going to be offended, but I think when you get well-known enough to have a parody made of your work, it's a compliment.

*

When the song was released on 11 February 1983, it went to number one in both the UK and the US and ended up spending an entire month at the top of the American charts. It also became the most successful single Jim Steinman had been involved with at that time. It sold over 60,000 copies in one day, which is amazing, and it's now nudging six million! I may have had to wait until I was thirty-two, but I felt like I'd done exactly what I'd set out to achieve. Robert threw a huge surprise party for me back home, which was wonderful. All my friends and family came, and we had a riot.

The number of records we used to sell was incredible. At the end of every day, I used to phone RCA and CBS and ask how many sales we'd had that day, and every single day it was at least 36,000 copies. I had many, many years of that and then when I did 'Total Eclipse of the Heart' those figures went sky-high. It was selling over 57,000 copies a day, which is unbelievable by today's standards, where it's all about downloads.

Because you could still make money by selling singles and albums before the digital world took over, record companies were very well-off, and the money was very rewarding for the artists too. You just don't make money from records anymore; it's all about touring, unless you're Ed Sheeran or Beyoncé or Adele. All the money comes from ticket sales and merchandise, whereas back then we were making money from hit records.

Now, I make new records because I want to have new material to perform on stage, or because I want a reason to do another tour (not that I ever need a reason!). But you don't make new music to make money. The music business has changed beyond all recognition.

I started working with Jim on my next album, so Robert and I decided to up sticks and move to New York for a while. We were staying in a lovely hotel overlooking Central Park, and we had a ball. We'd go cycling around Central Park together, and we were living the high life, going to fancy restaurants whenever I wasn't working. The hotel was beautiful, but neither of us expected to be staying there for so long. When the time came to pay the bill, I realised I could probably have bought an apartment for the same money!

Every Saturday night, Robert and I used to go to the most amazing Chinese restaurant called Mr Chow. It was near the Hudson River, and it was very glamorous. Andy Warhol was often in there with an entourage of models. There would be fourteen or fifteen of them around the table, looking achingly cool. It was known to be a bit of a celebrity hangout. I wasn't into star-spotting or anything, but you were always guaranteed to see someone you recognised. But we didn't go there because of that – we went because the food was so good. We loved sharing the cracked lobster with ginger and spring onion.

One night when we were in there, Robert said to me, 'Don't look around now, but Robert Wagner is sitting just behind you.'

Well, I will admit I *was* excited about that. Robert and I

used to watch *Hart to Hart* religiously, so I was dying to turn around and have a look.

When Robert Wagner got up to leave, he came over to our table and said, 'Bonnie, I'm with my daughter, and she doesn't like to ask you herself, but would you mind giving her your autograph?'

Bless her, this gorgeous young girl was too shy to come over and ask me herself. Of course, I gave him one. Then we had a brief chat, and they left. What a moment!

I'm not just saying this, but my husband Robert and Robert Wagner are dead ringers for each other. People have always said it, but I don't let it go to Robert's head! Still, the next thing we knew, a woman came up to our table and stood there, staring down at us. Someone must have told her that Robert Wagner was in the restaurant, because she said to my Robert, 'Would you mind giving me an autograph, Mr Wagner?'

I laughed and said, 'This is my husband. Mr Wagner has just left!'

He didn't say anything, but I think Robert was very flattered.

*

Once I started working on the album, it was like being in another world. The musicians were incredible, and there was such a good atmosphere in the studio. I had two members of Bruce Springsteen's E Street Band working with me: Roy Bittan, who was doing these great arrangements on piano, and Max Weinberg, who was incredible on drums. We also had Rick Derringer, a founding member of the band the

McCoys. He was known for these great guitar solos, like his amazing one on my version of 'Have You Ever Seen the Rain?'

The way Jim worked was incredible. He would do nine different takes of each song on reel-to-reel tapes, then take them home to listen to. He'd give me the cassette versions to do the same with. The following morning we would both come in saying which number track we thought was the best. And would you know, when we listened to all those recordings of 'Total Eclipse of the Heart', we both knew instantly it was going to be the second take. We looked at each other and said, 'Number two!'

I wanted to scream because the team were all so bloody fantastic, and it was such an honour to be in the same studio as them. It was all very collaborative, and we made such a great team. I was over the moon, and felt like I'd finally found the people I should have been working with all along. I'd always known that my voice was capable of handling these kinds of songs; it had just taken a while to convince everyone else!

Jim gave me so much confidence. He said that I was a great rock 'n' roll singer, but that I'd never had the chance to use my voice properly. We ended up using a lot of the guide tracks on the final album. A guide track is where you record a kind of demo, I guess, usually with just the rhythm section, to get a feel for the songs. But Jim didn't feel we could improve on my vocals, which was very flattering, so some of the guides ended up being used.

The album took three months to put together. Jim and I gelled so well, we probably could have done it quicker, but he would tell David and me so many fascinating stories over so many takeaways, and it was such a wonderful experience working with him that we enjoyed every single moment of our time there.

I did panic a bit when the album was released. I thought people might pick it up but then put it back on the shelf when they saw my face on the cover and realised who I was. The last time they had heard me, I was singing sweet country songs, and now I was back with this pop-rock album that would blow your socks off.

When I did the photo shoot for *Faster Than the Speed of Night*, I wanted the photos to be as good as they could possibly be. I've never been very good at doing the whole pouting thing. I'm not what you would call a 'natural' in front of the camera. Because of that, whenever I did press shots for single and album covers, whoever was shooting it had to take hundreds of pictures. Maybe I should have had a few red wines to relax me first. Or maybe not . . .

I did the photo shoot for the album in London, so I said to my hairdresser, Jan – or JJ, as I call her – 'I've got this photo session for my album in London. Would you come and do my hair?' She came up, and she did a great job, but she had to rush off because she had to get back home to Swansea to pick up her daughter from dance school. To this day, we still laugh about it. She always says, 'What was I thinking? Why the hell did I not stay for that iconic photo? Why didn't I arrange for someone else to pick up my daughter?' She did the same thing for the 'Total Eclipse of the Heart' video, and we laugh about that too.

I've never had any kind of entourage travelling with me, like make-up artists or hairstylists – it's just Robert, my manager, band and crew. I've always done my make-up myself, and I still do to this day. I do my own hair, too, and I still go to the same hairdresser back home as I went to in the seventies to get my colour done. JJ trained in London, and she's always, always done my hair colour. I get lots of compliments on it, so she must be good.

*

Off the back of the single being so big, the album had pre-sales of 90,000 in the UK. I was finally making the music I wanted to make, and music I was proud of – and it was shaking up the charts. It was more than I could have hoped for, and I felt like those two long years away from the music scene were worth it. All those times I had worried about whether I could make a comeback melted into the background. I officially found out my album was number one in the UK charts while I was staying in a lovely hotel in Leeds during a promotional tour. Dave Lee Travis – who was the first DJ to play 'Total Eclipse' on UK radio – phoned and told me the news live on Radio 1.

Robert, David and the radio plugger from CBS were in the room with bottles of champagne, and corks started popping. Dave Lee Travis asked me what I was doing, and I was so excited I said, 'I'm having a fuck's fizz!' instead of a Buck's fizz! Live on air! Oops! But it was such a great moment, and I was so happy that everyone was there to share it and celebrate.

I felt absolutely elated that I had a number-one album. A number-one single would have been great, but an *album*? I also made it into the Guinness World Records as the first woman to debut at number one in the UK Albums Chart. 'Total Eclipse of the Heart' grabbed people's attention, and I know that song has taken me to a new level of success that I didn't ever expect to achieve.

Jim sent me a huge bouquet of flowers to celebrate the success, and I felt like I was floating on air. He was just as happy as I was, and instinctively we knew that we had created something that would be talked about for years.

The album was also huge in America, where I battled for the number-one spot against Michael Jackson's *Thriller*, the Police's *Synchronicity* and Quiet Riot's *Metal Health* – and I won! The album went platinum status in the UK, America, South Africa, Sweden, Australia, Switzerland and New Zealand, to name but a few!

Faster Than the Speed of Night is the album that I guess you could say changed my life. I was already known over in America, but this was on a completely different level. Having a number-one album in America made me think, *I can't be too bad at this singing lark!* It was a huge lift for my confidence. I don't mean that arrogantly, like I suddenly thought I was something special; I just mean that it pushed me further outside my shy comfort zone. I was doing shows back to back, and I had to get out there and sing to huge crowds, no matter how shy or nervous I was feeling. It taught me that I can go out and perform, even if I'm standing backstage with my knees shaking, feeling a bit breathless. I learned that the fear of getting out on stage was more scary than actually being there.

I'd recorded some of the most iconic songs that were ever written with Jim Steinman for that album. I also toured America, which was amazing. But everything was so busy I didn't really have time to enjoy it. What with all the promotion and the travelling and performing, it all kind of blurred into one. It was only years later that I was able to appreciate it for what it was and see what an amazing experience it had been, and appreciate just how successful the album was. It was one of the most successful periods of my life career-wise, but I think it can be hard to see it when you're in it.

It changed my life in terms of how manic things were, but it certainly didn't change me as a person. I didn't let the success go to my head and start snapping my fingers at waiters in restaurants. I would be horrified with myself if I started acting like that! I was brought up to have manners, and I don't think being famous or successful means you're better than anyone else or that you can start treating people differently. I know that kind of behaviour does go on because I've seen it, but at the end of the day, you can be the biggest star in the world one week, and the next week someone else can come along, and no one gives a shit about you anymore!

I know there's that great saying, 'Be nice to everyone on the way up, because you'll meet them on the way down', but I wouldn't have dreamed of being rude to anyone, famous or not.

We all know that show business is a funny old world. You can go from the highest high to the lowest low in no time, and the thing that stopped me from losing my mind or getting above my station was knowing that it was a job, but it wasn't who I was. Inside, I will always be that fourteen-year-old watching Cher on *Top of the Pops* and thinking how amazing she was. I'll always be the eight-year-old who fed her gran's chickens. And I'll always be the daughter of my parents, who brought me up to be a good person and remember what's important in life.

Of course, being number one around the world was incredible. But did I suddenly start wearing designer clothes and loads of diamonds and only dining in the fanciest restaurants? Absolutely not. When Robert and I went back to Wales, we still went to our old favourite restaurants.

But like a lot of singers, I was always looking forwards and wondering what would be next.

*

I was nominated for two Grammys in 1983 for 'Total Eclipse of the Heart'. The awards were held at the Shrine Auditorium in Los Angeles, a huge venue that looked like something out of a movie. I was asked to perform 'Total Eclipse', which was very flattering, but I was dressed in a very tight leather mini-dress and very high heels. I had to start singing from the top of a staircase and walk all the way to the bottom, looking at the audience the entire time. All I kept thinking was, *I'm going to fall, I'm going to fall!* Thank god I didn't.

Someone told me that it attracted the largest Grammy Awards television audience ever, and that 51.67 million people tuned in. Can you imagine if I'd slipped and ended up with my legs in the air in front of tens of millions of people?

And, of course, because it was the Grammys, when I walked to the front of the stage, there were all these megastars sitting right in front of me. I mean, we're talking Michael Jackson, Diana Ross, Lionel Ritchie . . . you name the biggest stars of that time, and they were all there, looking right at me. Eek. It was so nerve-wracking but also a huge buzz, because I'd never done anything on that scale before.

The Grammys are the biggest music awards in the world, in my opinion, and to be nominated is a real badge of honour, even if I didn't win. Irene Cara beat me in the Best Pop Vocal Performance, Female category with her song 'Flashdance . . . What a Feeling', which is a great track. Michael Jackson was the biggest winner of the night, taking home eight Grammys, and the likes of the Eurythmics and Herbie Hancock also performed. Culture Club were named Best New Artist. I mean, what a night!

I've been to so many awards ceremonies over the years that it's easy to lose track of what happened when, but 1983 and 1984 were big years for me when it came to awards shows. I was nominated in the eleventh American Music Awards for Favourite Pop/Rock Female Artist alongside Stevie Nicks, Donna Summer and Pat Benatar. Pat won that one, and I wasn't at all upset because I was up against some pretty good competition! I was also up against Michael Jackson for Favourite Pop/Rock Song, would you believe? Not surprisingly, he pipped me to the post with 'Billie Jean'. He was the biggest pop star in the world at that time, so just being in the same category as him was quite something.

I was asked to record the theme tune for a James Bond movie in 1983, but I turned down the opportunity, because as soon as I heard the song, I knew it wasn't suitable for me. I mean, that would have been incredible. To record a Bond song is something every singer would like to do, but when I played the song to my manager and Jim, they both agreed it wasn't for me. It was such a shame. Another singer, Lani Hall, performed it instead. It's one of the few Bond songs that didn't become a hit, which is a shame because it really suited Lani's lovely voice, and it seemed unfair.

I've also been offered quite a lot of West End shows over the years, but I know I'm not an actress, so I turned those down too. I was offered *Blood Brothers* and *Hairspray*, amongst others, but I've never had any aspirations to act. I don't like making videos, let alone acting on a stage!

I've also got zero aspirations to become a reality star. I would be terrible at it. I've lost count of the number of times I've been asked to do *I'm a Celebrity . . . Get Me Out of Here!* It would be my worst nightmare. I've also been asked to go on *Celebrity Countdown* and *The Chase: Celebrity Special*. The thing is, though, when I get time off from work, I need to rest, so I can't fit everything in. I got asked to do *Celebrity Bake Off* recently, and I would love to have done that, but I was already booked in to do some gigs. If they ask me again and I'm free, I will definitely do it, so watch this space!

*

I was invited on to Terry Wogan's chat show, *Wogan,* for the first time in 1983, which was something that actually *did* impress my mother. It was *the* talk show to go on in those days, and my entire family were big fans of his. I ended up working with Terry a lot over the years. He was the most wonderful man, so kind and funny. He is so missed by everyone who knew him. He was a true one-off.

The first time I went on *Wogan,* believe it or not, Tina Turner was also a guest, which blew my mind. I had met her once before when we did a German TV show together. She was rehearsing when I walked into the studio in Germany, and she said to me, 'Bonnie Tyler!' and then started singing 'It's a Heartache' in her amazing voice. I was like, *Oh my god, there's Tina Turner, and she knows my name, and she's singing my song!* I'll never forget, she was wearing a white shirt and a pair of jeans, and she looked incredible. I couldn't believe how petite and dainty she was. I expected her to be tall in real life, but she was like a beautiful doll. I was totally transfixed by her.

I was thrilled I had the chance to meet her again on *Wogan*. Tina and I were in separate dressing rooms backstage, and I came out of my dressing room, all dressed and ready to go, and Tina walked out of hers at the same time. She looked at me, and I looked at her, and we both opened our mouths. I was wearing a red leather mini-skirt and a red biker jacket with black fishnet tights and high heels. Meanwhile, Tina was wearing a thin-strapped red leather mini-dress with black fishnet tights and high heels.

She said, 'Uh oh, somebody's got to change.'

I laughed and replied, 'I hope it's you, because I haven't got any other clothes with me!'

She smiled and said, 'Don't you worry about it,' and she went off and changed. I thought that was absolutely gorgeous of her. She had looked so stunning in that red dress, so I felt really bad. But then, she looked stunning in everything.

Meeting her was an amazing experience. I used to sing her song 'Nutbush City Limits' during one of my sets at the Townsman, and I would spend hours watching videos of her singing 'Proud Mary'. She was electric on stage. I remember when she covered the Beatles' song 'Help'; it was extraordinary. There will never be anyone like her ever again. She was astounding, and had this amazing presence that made her totally unique.

I was devastated when she passed away. I was on stage in Denmark just after I heard the news, and I dedicated a song to her. I was so overcome by emotion, I broke down in tears in front of everyone. I didn't expect to do that, but it really, really hit me. I had to carry on singing while I was crying with mascara running down my face, but I couldn't help myself.

The word 'legend' gets thrown around a lot these days, but Tina and Terry were both legends, just like Paul McCartney, Tom Jones, Mick Jagger, Rod Stewart and Elton John. Some people are in a class of their own. You can't always put your finger on why, but they've got that special *something*.

*

I rounded off 1983 in quite a random way by doing a duet with Shakin' Stevens. We did a Christmas-themed cover of Priscilla Bowman's 1958 hit, 'A Rockin' Good Way (To Mess Around And Fall In Love)', in December 1983. I agreed to do it because I loved the song, and it turned out to be very successful. It got to number five in the UK charts and number one in Ireland. It charted well all across Europe, actually. But it wasn't plain sailing behind the scenes.

On the day we went into the studio, Shaky wanted to record the song over and over again, and I wanted to go home and see Robert and relax. He insisted we carried on, and in the end I said to him, 'I've done it, and I'm off. I've done my bit so you can do yours again if you like.' And with that, I headed home. I did feel a bit bad, but I was so tired, and there's only so many times you can sing the same song in one day, you know?

We spoke the following day, and he apologised, explaining he could be a bit of a perfectionist. I understand that, but the version we had done sounded great. We've bumped into each other since, and it's been very amicable. I never act like a diva, but sometimes you've got to put your foot down, I say!

CHAPTER FIVE

It's a Heartache

After 'Total Eclipse' had been such a huge hit, Simon Bates said that the follow-up single should be my cover of Creedence Clearwater Revival's 'Have You Ever Seen the Rain?'. Jim did a fantastic arrangement of it for me, so it was completely different to the original.

You would think if it was a great cover and a Radio 1 DJ was all geared up to play the song and promote it, it would be a good idea to release it. It was common sense, surely? But no, the record label had other ideas. Even though we had secured airplay with Radio 1, which almost guaranteed you a hit, they decided they wanted to go with the title track, 'Faster Than the Speed of Night'. I thought it was the wrong decision, and it was a bit of a slap in the face for Simon Bates as well. All my instincts said it was the wrong choice, but the label wouldn't see my point of view and insisted we needed to go with another original song.

Their gamble didn't pay off. The song didn't get any airplay, so it didn't do very well, and I was gutted about that. *Really* gutted. I still perform 'Have You Ever Seen the Rain?' in my show, and I still love it, but I guess it's a little bit bittersweet because I know it would have been another hit for me.

Back then, DJs could make or break a song. Radio was much more about the music then. There are some brilliant

DJs around now, but it's as much about quizzes and them having fun as it is playing songs. Don't get me wrong, I think that's great too, but in the seventies and eighties, the DJs were at the top of the tree in the music industry. They were the ones you wanted on your side. Later on, things became a lot more about TV, and again the presenters were a big part of that. Noel Edmonds was incredibly supportive of me, which I am so grateful for. He introduced me during my first-ever appearance on *Top of the Pops*, and always used to call my single 'It's a Heartache', 'It's a Hard Egg', which really made me laugh.

*

I really wanted to work with Jim again on my next album. Why would I not want to? I'd had such a great experience with *Faster Than the Speed of Night*, but I didn't know if he would have the time to work with me on a full album because he was so in demand. Everybody in the rock world wanted to work with Jim. He was the ultimate.

At that time, Meat Loaf's *Bat Out of Hell* album had been in the British charts for five years. *Five years!* And that was mainly down to Jim's genius, as well as Meat Loaf's enormous talent, of course. It's mind-blowing.

When Jim agreed to work with me again, I was thrilled. I don't know if everyone who worked with him felt like this, but there was magic in the air when we collaborated. He made me feel like I was walking on air, and I never had a doubt that we would create something special again. Jim was busy working on another project so I had to delay working on the album for a while, but I knew it would be worth it.

The first song he wrote for the new album was called 'Ravishing', and he suggested that should be the title of the album too. I just couldn't see it myself. It felt like I had a lot to live up to! It just didn't feel very 'me', because I didn't ever see myself as a pin-up type. I was worried people might expect me to come out with a new sexy siren image, and that would have been my worst nightmare. I know I had an image change for *Faster Than the Speed of Night*, but 'Ravishing' was taking things a bit too far. In the end, we agreed to call it *Secret Dreams and Forbidden Fire*, which is a line taken from Jim's track, 'Loving You's A Dirty Job (But Somebody's Got To Do It)'.

Choosing the songs was a long job in itself. We had about a hundred songs in total, so we booked a rehearsal studio for a few weeks and went through them one by one, working out which ones would stay and which would go. I was never given tapes of Jim's songs, though – only ones written by other people. Jim only ever played his songs to you on the piano. I didn't ever have a demo of 'Total Eclipse of the Heart', for instance. He would play it, and I would learn it. It was a really different way to do things and felt very personal.

We used the same studio as last time, the Power Station in New York, and we worked with a lot of the same musicians. The first song I recorded was 'No Way to Treat a Lady', which was written by Bryan Adams. I loved the song of his I'd recorded on the previous album, so we asked him if he had anything new that could work for me again, and that was the one he suggested. He even came down to the studio to have a listen, which was a big deal for me because I'm such a fan, and he's got a tremendous voice. He said he loved the way I'd sung his track, and I was thinking, *If you'd only offer to do a duet on the album!* That would have been cracking.

Desmond Child wrote two songs for the album, 'Love is a Game' and 'If You Were a Woman (And I Was a Man)', and I loved them both. He is another mega songwriter; some of his best-known tracks are Bon Jovi's 'Livin' on a Prayer', Alice Cooper's 'Poison' and Ricky Martin's 'Livin' La Vida Loca'.

Recording the song 'Ravishing' was great because it's a really powerful one. Hulk Hogan later adopted it as his theme song, and he played it whenever he walked into an arena to fight. We recorded a slightly different version for him, where the song kicked off with a chorus of people chanting 'Hulk, Hulk, Hulk!' before it went into the main lyrics. The budget was so tight we went out on to the streets of New York and asked people if they wanted to be on the song. The people you hear on that track aren't trained or famous; they were probably popping out to get their lunch and ended up coming into the studio to appear on that track! It made me laugh to think that this mountain of a man used to walk into wrestling matches to my song.

I also did a cover version of the old Freda Payne song 'Band of Gold', the song that helped me get discovered, but we made it sound totally different by using synthesisers and a drum machine.

Todd Rundgren duetted with me on 'Loving You's a Dirty Job'. The song has typical Jim Steinman lyrics, because it's about two people who can't live with each other and can't live without each other. That old story! They love each other, but they can't stop fighting. Jim was so good at expressing how people felt in relationships (mainly bad ones!).

I recorded another song called 'Before This Night is Through', which I thought was great, but it didn't make the album. Jim's songs are so long we could only get eight on in total! 'Before This Night Is Through' was included on the cassette and CD versions, though. There's also another bonus song on the cassette and CD called 'Under Suspicion', which I co-wrote with Peter Oxendale, who played keyboards with Frankie Goes to Hollywood, and my brother Paul.

'Loving You's a Dirty Job' became the first release from the album. But, of course, what comes with singles? Videos. I had never once enjoyed making one. I always felt like saying, 'I'm a singer, not an actress!' Some people can do both, but I'm not one of them. It's funny that I'm comfortable on stage and I don't mind doing TV interviews, but I don't enjoy playing a character. I feel a bit ridiculous, really.

My manager, David, really wanted me to enjoy this video, so he got four different production companies to send over ideas and storyboards so I could see which one I felt most at ease with. We chose a video by a director called Tim Pope, who did a lot of work with David Bowie and the Cure, and I have to say, working with Tim was the first time I had ever enjoyed making a music video. He was such a nice guy, and he walked me through every bit of it, rather than expecting me to remember the entire storyboard, which would generally go in one ear and out the other! He was very patient and understanding.

Todd was busy when we had to do the shoot so he couldn't be in it. What I also liked about Tim's idea was that he didn't want Todd to appear as a silhouette, which all the other companies suggested. Instead, we hired an actor, Hywell Bennett, so it was very obvious that we weren't trying to pretend Todd was in the video. Hywell's lip-syncing was so good you would have sworn he was actually singing the words.

I have done a lot of duets in my time, and they've always been fun. When you're used to being a solo singer, it's nice having someone singing alongside you.

One of my favourite people to work with was the amazing Meat Loaf. We had a number-three album called *Heaven & Hell* back in 1989, which was a compilation album mainly made up of songs Jim Steinman had written. I also performed on stage with Meat Loaf a few times, and he was larger than life, as you would expect. He was very loud and never, ever boring. His bark was bigger than his bite, and he was good fun. He was the kind of person who you would know was in the room without having to turn around and look. He was a fascinating character. We recorded another duet together at the end of the nineties called 'A Kiss is a Terrible Thing to Waste'. Sadly, he had problems with his voice around that time, so the song got scrapped and didn't ever see the light of day.

'I Would Do Anything For Love' is probably my favourite Meat Loaf track. There was a rumour going around for years that I sang on that track, but actually, it was my good friend Lorraine Crosby. However, they used a model in the video who mimed Lorraine's part, which was really not on. You can understand how Lorraine would be very upset about that. Anyone would be. Lorraine didn't ever get any recognition for her part in the song, and her name wasn't even on the record. They called her 'Mrs Loud' instead of using her real name. If that happened these days, it would be called out on social media, and everyone would know about it, but I guess that says a lot about the music industry back then.

Lorraine has talked about it on TV a couple of times, but she should have been given the credit she deserved when she recorded it. It's so frustrating.

I never did ask Jim Steinman what the song was about and what it was that he wouldn't do for love, and now I'll never know. Maybe the answer is hidden in a vault somewhere, and one day we'll all find out. Until then, it will remain one of music's biggest mysteries.

*

Without a doubt, the biggest single to come from *Secret Dreams and Forbidden Fire* was 'Holding Out for a Hero', which has followed in the footsteps of 'Total Eclipse' by becoming a bit of an anthem. But it took a long time for it to get noticed.

The song originally came about a couple of years before the album, after Paramount Studios phoned my manager and asked if I'd be interested in doing a song for the film *Footloose*. Jim worked on the track with Dean Pitchford, an incredible Grammy and Oscar-winning songwriter, actor and screenwriter who wrote the screenplay for *Footloose*.

Before I recorded the song, I was invited to the Paramount film studios in Hollywood to view the rushes of the film so I had some idea of the action that was going to be taking place when the song was played. I needed to get a feel for the type of emotions I should put into my vocals, and it helped me get a sense of the energy needed to perform the song. We were in one of the tiny theatres you see in movies when a director is watching a preview of a film and deciding which bits to cut. It was a bit of a thrill being in a proper film-making studio with all these props around. I felt like a film star myself that day.

If you haven't seen the film yet, don't read the next paragraph. If you have seen the film and you want to be reminded of what happens, *do* read the next paragraph!

The story is about a city boy called Ren (played by Kevin Bacon) whose father dies, so his mother decides to move from Chicago to the country to be nearer her extended family. Ren meets a girl he likes, but she's already going out with a country boy. 'Holding Out for a Hero' comes in when the boys are having a competition to see who can stay on a moving tractor longest, essentially playing 'chicken' – clearly in an effort to impress the girl. Anyway, the two tractors are going hell for leather towards each other along a narrow ledge, and Ren gets his shoelace caught on the accelerator so he can't get off the tractor. The country boy doesn't realise what's happened, so he ends up jumping off his tractor first, so Ren wins and looks like a proper hero. There's so much tension in that scene, and I thought it was wonderful.

I went into a studio in LA the following day to record the song. The instrumental part was taken from a song called 'Stark Raving Love' on Jim's solo album, *Bad for Good*, and it was electrifying. I had some issues with my throat, so I was very concerned that I wouldn't do the best job I could. To be honest, I don't think I did. To this day, I still think I sing it better live than it sounds on the record. But what an opportunity to be given. I love belting it out.

There were four hit records off the *Footloose* soundtrack, but 'Holding Out for a Hero' wasn't one of them. It was first released as a single in January 1984, and it didn't chart very well, so we put it on the back burner and kind of forgot about it. About a year and a half later, Channel 4 began to play it as the theme music for their show *American Football* every Sunday. Then it started being used on an American soap opera called *Cover Up,* and suddenly people were going mad about it. They were going into record shops to try and buy it, but obviously there were no copies anywhere.

It became what's known as a 'sleeper hit', and the record company wasted no time in re-releasing it in August 1985. Within weeks, it was huge. I had no idea that the song had even been re-released until I got a phone call from CBS saying I needed to get to London asap so I could perform it on *Top of the Pops*. I was at the Hotel Parker Meridien in New York, and I remember that moment so clearly, because the hotel had a pool on the roof and Robert and I were up there sunbathing. Instead, I had to throw some things into a suitcase and get on the first plane to London!

The re-released single went to number one in Ireland and stayed at number two in the UK for three weeks, but it was kept off the number-one spot by Mick Jagger and David Bowie's Live Aid charity single 'Dancing in the Street'. Then Jennifer Rush released 'The Power of Love' and knocked them off the top spot, and I went down to number three. It was all about the power ballad back then, and I loved all the strong female voices in the charts.

'Holding Out for a Hero' became a bit of an anthem in gay bars, which of course, I loved. I've been told I'm something of a gay icon, but I'm not sure why. I'm flattered, nonetheless!

Filming the video for 'Holding Out for a Hero' was quite

an experience. We filmed in Arizona, and in one scene, I had to stand right on the edge of the Grand Canyon. There was a helicopter filming me from above, and the director, Doug Dowdle, said to me, 'Throw your arms up in the air, Bonnie, and let your dress blow in the wind!' I was waving my arms around like crazy, but it was so windy because we were up so high, and then there was the wind from the helicopter, and I was worried I might blow away. The man strapped to the side of the helicopter filming me must have had balls of steel!

The wind was so strong at one point it did actually blow me over, but thankfully backwards instead of forwards. The director said to me, 'Sorry Bonnie, we won't get so close next time,' and I replied, 'You won't have a bloody chance, mate, I'm moving further back.' All the speakers were hidden in the shrubs around me, so we had to move everything back a few yards and reshoot. It was so dangerous!

The rest of the video was almost as bizarre as the one for 'Total Eclipse of the Heart'. There were singers in white dresses, cowboys on horseback dressed head-to-toe in black and carrying neon whips, and another cowboy dressed in white, who represented my hero. It was quite camp. Perhaps the whole 'gay icon' thing shouldn't have come as such a surprise . . .

After failing to set the world alight the first time around, 'Hero' went on to do pretty well for itself. It was certified platinum in the UK in 2021, having sold over 600,000 copies. The great thing is that these days, younger people know the song because it has been featured in the films *Who's Harry Crumb?*, *Bandits* and *Shrek 2*, in which it was sung by the

Fairy Godmother, voiced by Jennifer Saunders. It means a whole new generation got to know it.

Adam Lambert recorded a cover of it recently, and you can imagine how brilliant it sounds with his voice. Jim Steinman would have loved it. It appears on Adam's album *High Drama*, and Heart Radio in America asked me to record an introduction for it that they could play to tie in with Pride. I thought it was such a lovely thing to do. Adam performed the song at his concert at Wembley in 2023, and apparently, he did a shout-out to me. Isn't that a fabulous thing? I had a hit with that song almost forty years ago, and now Adam Lambert's making it fabulous again. I have to say, I think he's incredible – and I wouldn't mind having a make-up lesson from him. What a beautiful man.

*

Jim and I had worked brilliantly together, but he was always incredibly busy. For that reason, I did my next album, my seventh, with Desmond Child.

As I said, he'd written two songs for my last album, but this entire album was produced by him. We called it *Hide Your Heart* – or *Notes from America* if you bought it in South or North America, because it was released under two different names. It was so fantastic to record, and much rockier than the music I'd made with Jim. It had a harder edge to it and sounded more like Bon Jovi or Cher, two artists Desmond has worked with a lot over the years.

We mainly recorded it at Bearsville Studios near Woodstock, New York, and the rest was done at The Hit Factory and Right Track, also in New York. Desmond made

the process a lot of fun, even though there were some challenges. My record company, CBS, were going through some
troubles at the time, so they only gave Desmond enough
budget for three songs. How were we supposed to make an
album out of that? But let me tell you, we did. He managed
to pull together a full track list of ten songs. The budget
was so tight that when we needed a large chorus of people
to appear on the opening song, 'Notes From America', we
went out on to the streets of New York and asked people if
they wanted to be on the album. The people you hear on
that song aren't trained or famous; they were probably
popping out to get their lunch and ended up coming into
the studio to appear on that track!

The other title track, 'Hide Your Heart', was written by
Desmond, Holly Knight and Paul Stanley, the co-lead vocalist
and guitarist from Kiss, and it was originally going to be
recorded for Kiss's album *Crazy Nights*. They eventually
included it on their next album, *Hot in the Shade*, the year
after my album came out.

We had such amazing writers involved in that album.
Holly Knight was the genius who wrote Pat Benatar's 'Love is
a Battlefield', which is such a classic. Holly Knight and Mike
Chapman also wrote a song called 'The Best', which I loved. I
wanted it to be my first single release from the album. It was
originally written for a male artist, but he passed on it, so I
got to record it. It was such a cracker I couldn't help but think
he must have been mad.

There were some more soulful numbers too. Michael
Bolton and Desmond wrote a track called 'Take Another Look
at Your Heart', and we also had 'Save Up All Your Tears', which

balanced out some of the tougher-sounding songs on the album.

I recorded a Janis Joplin song, too, 'Turtle Blues', completely by mistake. We happened to finish recording the album the same day Jimmy Barnes came in to record his next one. (He's had twenty number-one albums in Australia, would you believe?) Desmond and Jimmy started jamming, and Jimmy began to sing 'Turtle Blues', which Janis had written when she was in the band Big Brother and the Holding Company. The studio had a copy of the record, so I started singing along while two amazing guys from Jimmy Barnes's band, bass guitarist Seth Glassman and lead guitarist John McCurry, played the music for me. They decided to swap instruments to make the record sound even more raw, and we ended up finishing the recording at 2am. When I found out that Janis had recorded the original in that very studio, I was lost for words. Having been a fan of Janis's for so long, it was a truly breathtaking moment.

Desmond decided it had to be on the album, so it was a last-minute addition. It's one of my favourite songs of all time, let alone that I've recorded. I do it at my shows, and it's always received really well. It's completely different to the rest of the show because it's a blues track, but it goes down a storm. It's so funny that it ended up on the album by a total fluke.

I also randomly ended up doing some backing vocals for Cher while Desmond and I were recording. He'd been working with her and producing some of her tracks, and he asked if I would sing on one of her songs. I was more than happy to. I can't for the life of me remember the name of the song, but it was an honour. I didn't get to meet her, and I still haven't to this day, but she did send me a gigantic bouquet of flowers to say thank you.

I nearly ended up with another very famous song on the album, too, courtesy of Jim Steinman. He happened to be renting a house very near to where I was recording, and he invited me, Robert and David Aspden over to have a meeting so he could play me a song. The track was called 'It's All Coming Back to Me Now'. I loved it, but the record company told me it was too expensive to work with Jim Steinman again. I knew it would be a massive hit, but they wouldn't budge. I was so sad, but I had to say no to Jim.

If any of you recognise the song title, you'll know that Celine Dion ended up recording it – and she *did* have a massive hit with it! She is an amazing artist, but I do think back even now and wonder if I should have paid the money myself and recorded it off my own bat. It's not a regret as such, because it just wasn't meant to be, but I can't help but think about it whenever I hear it.

*

I had taken some time out before the release of *Hide Your Heart* because things had been so busy and I needed a bit of a break. So I was looking forward to coming back with a bang when it was released in May 1988.

I knew it was a good album because you get a feel for these things. There have been times when I've recorded songs and I've got a feeling in my gut that they're not right or they don't suit my voice. But I liked every single song on that album, and I knew how talented Desmond was, so I thought we were on to a winner. What could possibly go wrong?

As it turns out, quite a lot . . .

What I didn't know was that during that time, CBS in America was going through some kind of court case that involved my UK record label, Sony. Something big was happening, and there was a lot of going back and forth. They weren't working together properly, and communication was bad because there had been some kind of fall-out. My album release got stuck right in the middle, along with singles and albums from a few other acts.

I don't know exactly what was going on, but because of the dispute, my record company was having a very hard time getting their songs played on the radio. I did a nineteen-date tour in the UK to support the album and it got some great reviews. *Music & Media* named it one of their Albums of the Week and said, 'With her powerful, raucous voice, the British rock singer delivers a pleasant album full of hook-heavy material, pompous build-ups and dramatic grooves.' So many people loved *Hide Your Heart*, but it wasn't getting any airplay, and it wasn't promoted in the way it should have been, which is such a shame. It just wasn't visible enough. To this day, I think it should have done better. My best chart position was in Norway, where it got to number two. I wish I could go back in time and change the way the album was handled. I would happily have done the promotion myself if they had told me upfront the record company weren't going to do any! There was no push behind it whatsoever. The only good thing to come out of it was that I'd shown I was right to trust my instincts with the songs because, clearly, they were good choices.

There were a lot of huge hit records on that album, but not

a single one of the hits happened for me. I had recorded them as original tracks before other artists recorded them, but for one reason or another, my versions didn't chart. For example, Robin Beck had a hit with 'Save Up All Your Tears' in 1989. Cher also recorded it and released it in 1991, and that did very well too. And the song I mentioned called 'The Best'? That's often better known as 'Simply the Best', and just two years later Tina Turner recorded it and had a stonking great hit. The only place my version of the single was released was in Norway, and while it became a top-ten hit, it didn't quite reach the dizzy heights that Tina's did. For my role model to have a monster hit with the track was bittersweet, but I was glad it did so well for her. Mine and Tina's paths crossed a lot, both musically and in person, and I feel very blessed about that.

I also recorded a few covers on *Hide Your Heart*, but again other artists went on to have more success with them. I did a version of Diane Warren's 'Don't Turn Around', which Tina Turner had also recorded as a B-side for her 1986 hit, 'Typical Male'. In 1988, Aswad had a number one with it, and Ace of Base later had huge success with their version. Then there was 'To Love Somebody', which was written and originally recorded by the Bee Gees. That was an old song I used to do on stage anyway. Then Jimmy Somerville covered it and reached the top ten. Safe to say that album was not my lucky charm!

*

I can't claim that 1988 was all bad, though, because I became one of the first female artists ever to tour Russia.

It was a real eye-opener because their lives were so different. The way the people out there lived was like nothing I'd ever seen. There would be these old women outside clearing the snow with a shovel, and it would break my bloody heart to see them because it was below freezing out there. The Russians had to queue for everything, and if you ordered a cup of tea with milk in a hotel it was a really big deal, and you'd have to wait for ages for it to come. I can't imagine what it was like living like that every day.

I played at the Kremlin Palace several times, and it's a stunning place. My first performance in Russia was at the Olympic Stadium in Moscow, and the first thirty rows of the crowd were made up of police. Everybody else in the audience had to be on their best behaviour – no jumping around, no screaming, none of the things that you'd normally expect at a concert. They all just sat there, and if anyone in the crowd stood up or did anything to show any form of enthusiasm, they were told off by the police. I wouldn't have risked doing anything I shouldn't have been if I were them.

I mean, how are you supposed to enjoy a concert under those conditions? They were the politest audiences I've ever had, and it was a truly strange experience. I'm used to people waving their arms about and singing along to my songs at the tops of their voices, but there was none of that.

Thankfully, I took catering with me, which was the best thing I could have done. The catering company were fantastic, and the Russian and Polish crew were stunned because I don't think they had ever eaten like that in their life. It made for a great atmosphere because everyone was so happy. I also took so many toiletries with me that I was giving them away at the end of the tour to the people that were taking care of me, and they were so thrilled.

I can't believe how much Russia has changed from then to now. Once communism ended, it went from one extreme to the other so quickly. It felt like, in a blink of an eye, Moscow was filled with designer shops and restaurants, and there were British brands everywhere. It was barely recognisable. Now, of course, because of the war, it's changed all over again, because so many brands and corporations won't have anything to do with Russia. It must be awful for all the people living there, and so incredibly unsettling and upsetting to see their home country go through such huge changes all over again.

I've got a Russian godchild called Paul whom I keep in touch with. His mother, Irena, was one of the ladies who was looking after me while I was out in Russia for that six-week tour. She also looked after me in later years when I went over there to play more concerts, and we became good friends. When she first asked me to be godmother to Paul, I said no, because I had so many godchildren already. But in the end, I caved, and it was a lovely experience being in that stunning cathedral.

When I say I've got a lot of godchildren, I'm not exaggerating. Dean (my sister Avis's son) and Daniel (Robert's step-brother Paul's son) are my godsons. I've got my friend Sue's daughter, Charlie, I've got Paul, and I've got a half-Portuguese and half-Ukrainian goddaughter called Leonor. I'm also godmother to Melanie, who is the daughter of my old school friend Christine.

I'm not having any more, though. I've got to say no. I'm

seventy-two now, and you can't ask a seventy-two-year-old to be a godmother. I don't always feel that I'm everything a godmother should be. I'm away travelling so much, and I am so short on time when I'm not working that I don't get a chance to see them all as much as I would like to, which is such a shame. I've also got sixteen wonderful nieces and nephews, who have all gone on to do amazing things with their lives, and, at the last count, about fourteen great-nieces and great-nephews. We are an ever-expanding family. It's huge! It was pretty big when I was growing up, but I don't think you'd get everyone around a Christmas dinner table now.

*

I was also one of the first Western artists to play in the UAE. This was before Dubai and other places became cool, popular places to go for holidays. I mainly worked in Bahrain, and I remember walking down the street, and people were stopping and staring at me because I had my shoulder out. They were looking at me like I was doing something really wrong. It made me realise that when you're in other people's countries, and they have rules, you have to adhere to them. I would never wear a hijab or cover myself, but it's a respect thing, isn't it?

After that, I was a lot more careful. I was probably a bit more naive back then, but it has also changed a lot now. Women wear bikinis on the beach in Dubai, and you can drink alcohol in certain places, which would never have happened in the days when I was there.

When you're in the public eye, you're always told not to talk about religion or politics in interviews, and I do stick to that rule because it only takes one word to get you into trouble. But I will say that I think people are entitled to believe what they believe. Just because something doesn't align with your values or beliefs, it doesn't mean it's wrong. I wear a Peace Mala bracelet, which promotes friendship, respect, and peace between all faiths and beliefs, to show that I respect everyone's religious decisions.

Right . . . now I'm going to step away from being controversial in any way, because it's not my thing!

CHAPTER SIX

Back Home

After our horrible Christmas Eve experience in our lovely house all those years ago, thankfully, we lived there happily and drama-free for the next sixteen years. We moved from there in 1988 when we bought our current house, which needed a lot of work doing to it. It was built in 1850, so it's very beautiful, with high ceilings and a lot of the original fittings, but it was a complete wreck. We spent two years getting work done on it because it had to be completely refurbished it. Roof, floors, walls – you name it. We enjoyed having that time to do it all up and make it all exactly how we wanted it.

When I was a young girl, I had a best friend called Diane. My parents couldn't drive, but her parents had a Morris 1000, and they loved taking us out for rides on the weekend, either to the beach or up to the Brecon Beacons, and I thought it was the best thing ever. Diane didn't love it as much as I did, but her mother, father and I would sing the whole time because we were so happy. When we used to drive to Mumbles, I used to pass a house that I loved. It always looked so lit up and had a conservatory, and I used to think, 'Oh my God, how I'd love to live there.' Little did I know that the big house next door with the really long drive was the one that Robert and I would end up buying in 1988!

Once the house renovations were finished, Robert and I started a tradition of holding Christmas parties every year, and people loved them. We used to get the biggest tree we could find, and Christopher, Lynn's wonderful son, who lives with us, would help me get out all the decorations. We'd put on Christmas music and decorate the house from top to bottom. Christopher is much more creative than me, so I would hand the decorations to him, and he would put them where they needed to go.

We would invite about 200 people along to a party every Christmas. It would be friends and the people from the wine bar down the road – anyone who wanted to come was welcome. I always hired catering because I didn't want to spend all my time in the kitchen – I wanted to catch up with everyone. Plus, I don't think I'll be winning *MasterChef* anytime soon, so it was probably for the best.

The party would start at around 11am on Christmas morning and end at around 5pm. In between, people would have nibbles and drinks, and we'd all sing around the piano. It was wonderful. People loved starting their Christmases off at our place, and we loved having them.

We did it for years and years, but when Covid kicked in, it all came to an end, and I miss it. During lockdown, when Robert and I were in Portugal, Christopher was at the house with his partner, John, and they decorated like normal. He sent me some wonderful photos, and it did tug at my heart-strings, making me wish I was there with a full house, having fun. It was one of the highlights of my year.

*

One of the best things I've been able to do throughout my whole career was to buy my parents a house, which felt like the biggest thank you for everything they did for all of us. Until then, they had lived in our childhood home, so I think it was a bit of a wrench at first, but it changed their lives.

Their new cottage was only a mile down the road from our house, so I got to see them all the time. My family has always remained close, and every time I go home, I try to see as many of them as possible. It's one of the things I look forward to most. Give me all the hits you like, but offer me a cup of tea and some cake with one of my brothers or sisters or a close friend, and I'm in heaven.

My mother loved our house, and she and my father used to come and stay there whenever I was away on tour, so we always knew it was safe. It's got lovely gardens, and we'd often have the family round for barbecues. My mother would be up with all the kids, playing bat and ball. She always used to beat them, even when she was in her seventies.

She really loved Robert. She loved all her sons-in-law, in fact. She thought the sun shone out of their backsides. She also adored my father – and he thought the absolute world of her.

*

Tragically, my mother started suffering from Alzheimer's when she was in her seventies. It's such a dreadful disease. I wouldn't wish it on anyone. It's heartbreaking to watch someone go through that, and I pray to God that no one else in my family gets it.

To watch someone you love more than anything become

147

someone who doesn't recognise you anymore is indescribable. I think it's the cruellest thing in the world, and I well up just thinking about it even now.

All of us kids were so close to her. Of course, we leaned on each other and our partners and also tried to support our father as much as possible, but nothing can make it better. You know that person is going to get increasingly worse. Some days my mother would recognise me, and other times she wouldn't have a clue who I was. She didn't know what was happening a lot of the time. Occasionally, she would look around at her surroundings at her house or mine, and she would say, 'Oh, I'm home!'

I will never forget a conversation we had one day just before Christmas, shortly before she passed. She was in my house, sitting by the kitchen table. I'd bought some red cotton napkins at the local fete with Father Christmas's face embroidered on. They were folded into triangles on the placemats, and she picked one up and folded it again and again until it became a tiny little triangle. She held my hand with hers and said, 'Gaynor, when I go . . .'

I said to her, 'Oh Mammy, please don't talk like that.'

We were both tearing up, and then she said, 'Will you put this in my coffin? I want to have something with me that I can give to Pauline.'

Pauline was my sister who was stillborn. My mother never got over that. Pauline was her fourth child, and she went to full-term with her, so she had to go through the trauma of the birth. It affected her so badly, as it would anyone. In those days, they didn't show the parents the child or let them hold them. To her dying day, my mother regretted never being able to hold Pauline in her arms and say a proper goodbye.

The doctors said there was nothing obviously wrong with Pauline, so she never did get any answers as to why it had happened and that made things so much worse. My parents held a funeral for Pauline, and she was buried in the grave-yard of the same local church where we all got married. Her grave is still there today.

My mother spoke about her all the time, and when people asked her how many children she had, she used to say she had seven, because she always included Pauline.

It broke my heart when she gave me this napkin, because even though her illness was bad by then, she could still remember the pain of losing my older sister.

As her illness progressed, Mammy had to go into hospital to learn how to use machines to help pull her up from bed and make her more independent so as to take some pressure off my father. She was only supposed to be in there for two weeks, but she didn't ever come out. It was terrible.

It took me years and years and years to get over her passing. Not that you ever really get over it – you just learn to cope. I was in a terrible state for a long time. We all were. She loved us so much, and nothing materialistic was of any comfort. You can buy all the things in the world, and none of it will make you happy if you're missing someone so badly.

You have to remember the good times. It's the only way. I always think about my mother singing and how much she adored us all. I try to remember all the wonderful things we did together, although of course I do still have my moments where I cry and miss her and my father.

At my mother's funeral, we all put something into her coffin, like a keepsake, a letter or a note for her. I kept my promise, and I put in the red Father Christmas napkin for Pauline too. I've still got one of the napkins from that set in a drawer at home, and every time I see it, I am reminded of that day. It was those moments of lucidity that made my mother's illness so hard. Sometimes you knew the old her was still in there, while other days it was like she didn't seem to remember anything about her life. She would smile and chat to me, but it was like talking to a stranger.

My mother died in 2001, two months before my fiftieth birthday. Robert was going to buy a boat for my birthday and have a party, but nothing in the world can make you happy when you're grieving, so I postponed everything and had a quiet celebration instead. My father phoned me on my birthday, and when I put the phone down, I had a good cry because it was the first time my mother hadn't been able to sing me 'Happy Birthday'.

I have so many wonderful memories of my parents, but there are two things my mother said that always stand out to me. The first was, 'Believe in yourself, because no one else is going to do it for you.' I've never forgotten that. If my confidence wavers even slightly, I'll think about those wise words. She also used to say to all of us kids, 'Keep the family tight.' Then she would hook one finger over the other to show us what she meant.

She had a leather bag that she kept all her life. It had old photos in it as well as our school reports and even love letters from my father. When she passed away, we looked for it everywhere. To this day, we still can't find it, and I'm devastated. We wonder if she did something with it one day when she was unwell, like throw it away or bury it in the garden. Maybe we'll never find it, and I'm so sad because it held so many memories.

*

Robert bought me the boat the following year, and my father came down to the shipyard in Plymouth with us to see it being built. I'll never forget him kissing the side of it, and then he named it for me. I wanted to call it something after my mother, but I didn't want to call it *Elsie*, because it seemed like a funny name for a boat. Quick as a flash, my father said, 'Call it *Angel*, because that's what your mother was.' It was perfect.

We went on a test drive on an identical boat to mine the same day, a Princess 50. Everything was exactly the same as it would be on mine, and I got some lovely pictures of my father on there. He was smiling from ear to ear.

We recently sold the boat, but we had a good twenty-one years of really great times on it – and a couple of scary ones too. One afternoon, the boat was moored in the marina in Portugal, and Robert was zooming back on the three-seater jet-ski with two of my little nephews. I saw them coming, so I thought I'd stand on the end of the boat and wait for them, but I slipped and ended up underneath it. I hadn't learned to swim by then because it wasn't some-thing I'd done as a child, and I'd been putting it off and putting it off, so I was flailing around, and Robert was terrified. I don't remember much about it, but he says I was under the water with my mouth open. He was trying to pull me out, but I was soaked through, so I was like a dead weight. Eventually, he got me up on to the boat and turned me over and patted my back, and I was fine. I was laughing hysterically; looking back, it must have been due to shock.

*

Anyone who has ever had a relative who has been through Alzheimer's always has it in the back of their mind that it might happen to them, because it can be genetic, so I think my siblings and I all wondered if we may also suffer with it when we were older.

I got some reassurance when I was around sixty-five, as a result of another accident on the boat. I was walking up the flybridge to the automatic door, and it came down on my head. It was a really heavy door, so I was totally dazed. We were just about to go and meet some friends, so I said I'd be okay and off we went.

I started getting bad headaches in the weeks afterwards, so Robert suggested I go for a brain scan. The good news is, they found one! The other good news is that the specialist told me there was nothing to worry about, which was such a relief.

He showed me my brain on his computer screen, in slices, so I could see exactly what it looked like, which felt very strange. The specialist showed me one slice and said it was very interesting because if there was any sign of Alzheimer's, there would be white spots on it, but there was nothing at all.

I said, 'I can't tell you what a relief that is.' *Then* he told me

I had the brain of a forty-five-year-old, which I was very pleased about.

I've always had quite a good memory, but I am bad at names and faces. I can be introduced to someone and have a long chat with them and by the end of the conversation I've forgotten what they're called. It's always so awkward when you then have to introduce them to someone, because what do you say? I often rely on Robert to remember for me.

One of the most embarrassing things that's ever happened to me was when we went out for dinner with Robert's accountant and his wife. We had a wonderful time, and they came back to our house afterwards for drinks. The following day, this woman came up to chat to me while I was shopping in M&S, and I just couldn't place her. I knew I had met her before, but I couldn't think where.

She said to me, 'Oh, wasn't it a fantastic night? It was so much fun.'

I think you can guess the punchline . . .

She looked at me a bit confused and said, 'Gaynor, we were out for dinner together last night!'

I didn't even recognise her from the *night before*. I must have been drunk, but even so, that's got to be one of my worst moments.

I really don't mean to be rude, and it comes down to seeing so many faces all the time. I meet so many people through work, and I seem to have a bit of a blind spot with remembering where I've met people and what they're called. If Robert wants to wind me up a bit, he'll say, 'Come on, Gaynor, you must remember so-and-so?' right in front of them, knowing full well I won't. As soon as it clicks, it clicks, but some people must think I'm terribly rude.

*

Sadly, my father only lived for about eighteen months after my mother passed on. My siblings and I always said that he kind of gave up after my mother died. He loved her so much, and I don't think he knew what to do without her. He wasn't interested in living once she had gone. They were married for over sixty years, and that's all he knew.

My mother never wore a scrap of make-up, and he always thought she was so beautiful. She always did her hair, and then she would pinch her cheeks to make them look rosier, and he used to laugh at that. Much like my Auntie Kate, my mother always wore heels, but hers were midheels, rather than Auntie Kate's towering ones. When my parents passed, I took their favourite pairs of shoes, and I keep them under my bed so I feel like they're always with me.

My father went to stay with my older sister Marlene and her husband Gwyn for a while so they could take care of him after my mother passed, but after six weeks, he said he wanted to go home because he felt like that's where he belonged. He was always very independent. We all helped out by looking after him and making sure he had enough food and that his bills were paid, but he was very good at taking care of himself.

The last time I saw my father, it was lovely, and we had loads of kisses. We dropped him off at the Castle Hotel in Neath on our way to the airport, because we were heading back to Portugal. He was heading off to meet what was left of his old friends for a couple of half-pints, and he said, 'Have a wonderful time, you two. You really deserve it.' I gave him a big hug and told him I loved him, not knowing that would be the last time I would ever see him alive.

I feel so lucky I've got those lovely last memories of him being full of smiles and happy. He was in his mid-eighties, but he didn't look it and was always dressed immaculately. He still had plenty of life and spirit in him, even at that age.

Not long after that, my sister Angela was supposed to pick him up one Wednesday so she could take him for his weekly trip to the Castle. This particular Wednesday, my sister was ringing and ringing his phone to arrange what time to collect him, and there was no answer. She couldn't understand it, so she called my nephew Christopher and asked him to pop down to the house. He arrived at around 10am and knocked on the door, but there was no answer.

Christopher looked through the letterbox, and he could see that the lights were on, but my father wasn't answering. In the end, he called the fire service so they could smash down the door, because something obviously wasn't right. They found my father in the downstairs bathroom, and said straight away that he had passed. He had suffered a brain aneurysm, so the positive thing is that he would have died quite quickly.

Chris called me in Portugal to tell me the news, and I was broken. When you've been lucky enough to have your parents for so long, you know it's inevitable that phone call is going to come one day, but when it does, it shakes you to your core nonetheless.

Robert and I flew straight home, and when I saw him in the open coffin, he didn't look like himself at all. He had always been such a gorgeous man, but because of the post-mortem he looked puffy and bloated. It was very upsetting, because that's not how I remembered him.

I don't let myself think about it now. Instead, I always think back to him waving and smiling as we drove away from the Castle.

*

I remember Cilla Black always used to say, 'I only turn left on a plane.' But if I'm going to Portugal, I don't care if I go on Ryanair or easyJet or whatever, because it's only a short flight. If I'm travelling further, I will fly business class or club class, which is a real treat. It's usually because I need to be rested for a show.

I'll never forget flying back from New York once. Robert and I were in business class. On either side of us were these two big burly men; I assumed they were someone's body-guards. One of the cabin crew asked if they were mine, and I said, 'You're joking, aren't you? I've got my husband here; he's my bodyguard!'

These guys were the proper business with smart suits and sunglasses – the works. After take-off, I put up the partition so I could have a bit of privacy, but after a short while, it started going back down. I thought it was the cabin crew bringing me more champagne, so I held my hand out because I was very happy.

I looked up to see Mariah Carey! She was absolutely gorgeous. She said to me, 'Hi Bonnie, I've just been told you're on the flight, and I wanted to come and say hi.'

I was like, 'Oh my *god*, it's so lovely to meet you.'

We talked for ages, and she told me she used to sing my songs when she was a young girl. It was so lovely to hear that. We've got completely different types of voices, so I'd love to have heard how her sweet vocals sounded on 'Total Eclipse'. She is the most incredible singer, but we couldn't be more different! I thought it was wonderful. After a while, she swapped seats with the bodyguard who was sitting on the seat next to me so we could chat more.

She had her first-class pyjamas on and no make-up, but she looked stunning. We chatted for ages and ages, about everything from the industry to different songs we loved, and she was so friendly and sweet. She was nothing like this big diva everyone makes her out to be.

At one point she looked confused and said, 'Bonnie, where's your entourage? Where are they?'

When I said I only travelled with my husband, band and manager, she looked stunned.

Honestly, she couldn't believe it. Then she leaned forward and said in a quiet voice, 'You know when you're on long-haul flights and you've got to work straight away – like, the minute you get off the plane – are you able to sleep on flights? How do you manage it?'

'Well,' I said, 'what I do is, I go to my doctor, and I say, "I'm going on a long-haul flight. Can you give me two sleeping tablets, for me and my husband?" We each take a half on the way out and a half on the way back.'

She explained she could never sleep on a flight, and I said, 'Funnily enough, I've got a spare sleeping tablet here if you want it, but only take half of it.' I handed her the pill, and she only went and took the whole bloody thing!

We carried on talking for about an hour, and she looked like she was starting to fall asleep. I said, 'Mariah, you had better go back to your seat in first class, or you'll fall asleep right here!'

The next thing you know, her bodyguards came and escorted her back to her bed. They were practically carrying her because she was so woozy. I thought, *You silly bugger, taking the whole tablet!*

When the plane landed, I went to the door, and the special assistance team were there. They're the crew who help celebrities get on and off planes. One of them said, 'Oh, hi Bonnie, we must be here for you?' and I replied, 'Oh no, it will be Mariah. Mariah Carey's on the plane.' She must have still been sleeping.

The next day, I was in bed watching *This Morning* with Fern Britton and Phillip Schofield, and who should pop up but Mariah! During the interview, she said, 'I flew in from New York last night, and I met one of my idols on the flight.' They asked who it was, but she refused to say in case the person in question didn't want to be mentioned. I was sitting in bed shouting at the screen, 'Tell them! Tell them it was me!'

Then I thought, *Actually, maybe it's best if she doesn't. I don't want her telling them that she ended up zonked out for the entire flight because I gave her a sleeping tablet.*

I haven't seen her since, but I can honestly say she was so sweet. She was hugely famous by then as well, so it's not as if she was a newcomer. I thought she was wonderful.

*

Getting recognised is quite normal to me now, but not by the likes of Mariah Carey! The first time I realised people knew who I was came after 'Lost in France' had been a hit. I went into a chemist in Swansea, and the lady serving me said her daughter would want to know what I was buying – that was a strange one.

I remember in the early days, before mobile phones, people would come up and say hello, and 99.9 per cent of the time, they were supportive, but not *everyone* was nice. Shortly after 'Lost in France' came out, I was in a bar waiting to get served. The girl standing next to me had just got her drink, and she handed me her change and said, 'Here you go, love. You're probably a one-hit wonder, so you'll be needing this.' What a horrible thing to do. If only I knew who she was. I'd go and knock on her door and give back her change!

If I am recognised, I'll always stop and say hello. I know some artists don't like it, but I don't mind at all. I never go out without my make-up anyway, because it's a part of me, so at least I look half-decent in selfies. I don't want to be all over Instagram looking like shit!

I'll never forget my eldest sister, Marlene, saying to me when I was young, 'When you get married, always look nice for your husband.' It feels very old-fashioned now, but the idea has always stuck in my head – with one key difference. I like to look nice for myself. It's how I am.

I've had a few style changes over the years, but I'm not sure I'd call them reinventions as such. Some have been very natural progressions and have been what I've wanted to do.

The thing is, I'm not really into fashion – I just wear what suits me, which is mainly jackets and jeans, and I've worn the same kind of clothes ever since I moved away from country-pop music. Leather was my go-to in the eighties. I couldn't get enough! But I calmed things down in the nineties. I still wore a lot of black clothes, and I loved patent boots, but leather is very heavy, and you grow out of these things, don't you? That's not to say I've ditched it altogether. I still love a leather jacket and a bit of fringing when it's called for, but I'm not sure I could do an entire gig dressed in leather trousers again. My goodness, they're hot.

My hair has changed a bit over the years too. At first I wore it straight, then in curls in the eighties, and now I'm back to a straight style.

I don't think I'll ever truly get used to it, even after all these years, but it's very flattering that people want to say hi. I don't go out hoping to get recognised, but I don't fear it either. If I did, I'd end up being a bloody hermit. The only thing I won't do is sunbathe on a beach, because I don't want to be all over Facebook or Instagram in a bikini. It would be my worst nightmare to pick up a newspaper and see a photo of me in all my glory!

The funniest thing is if I catch someone's eye or they recognise me in a restaurant. When I go to the toilet, you can bet they'll follow me in. I'll be brushing my hair in the mirror, and they'll say, 'It is you, isn't it? Is it you?' Quite often, people will say to me, 'My god, you look so much like Bonnie Tyler, only younger.' Obviously, I love that! Keep those comments coming!

I also get recognised by my voice quite often. I guess I have one of those voices that is distinctive. When I've phoned up to book restaurants before, people have said, 'You sound just like Bonnie Tyler!' I've even had people turning around in shops saying, 'I knew it was going to be you!'

There have even been a couple of people who have pretended to *be* me over the years. My manager, David, called me about twenty years ago and asked me how I knew John Cale. He was another Welsh musician who co-founded the Velvet Underground. I said that I'd never met him in my life, and David told me there was a chapter in John Cale's memoir all about me and something very rude I'd apparently done in a flat in London years before. In the end, I had to go to court and get the chapter removed, because it certainly wasn't me! I won the case, and I got awarded some money, which I gave to charity. It wasn't about the payout at all; I just wanted my name cleared. I can only think he must have been duped by an imposter. Judging by the story, someone who looked very much like me must have been a bit of a party girl in her time!

There was another rumour that I was once spotted in a South Wales pub wearing nothing but a fur coat, and I had dyed my pubic hair green. I mean, can you imagine? Do me a favour; it's ridiculous!

I remember seeing a different girl in Swansea when I was in my late twenties who was the double of me. She was also called Gaynor, so it's no wonder people were confused when they met her. My best friend, Gloria, was in the Valbonne club one night, and she overheard the other Gaynor telling some bloke she *was* me. Gloria went straight over there and set the record straight. So maybe I've got a few lookalikes around?

Speaking of Gloria, she was the most *amazing* person. Our friendship lasted right up until she sadly passed away two years ago. It's still very hard to talk about now. She was with me throughout everything, and I miss her terribly. She was such a beautiful person. I still get emotional thinking about her. She was like another sister. I didn't feel like I got to say a proper goodbye to Gloria when she died because, without anyone's knowledge, she had arranged to be cremated straight away. She didn't have a funeral. Even though it was totally up to her what she did, I found that very hard. I wanted a proper way to honour her, so I got all our friends together, and we celebrated our darling Gloria's life. The only thing missing was her.

She was an amazing friend to Robert too. We talk about her a lot, which is sad, but also lovely. It's nice that we can remember the good times.

Robert and I share a lot of mutual friends, and I feel lucky that I've never had to worry about whether I can trust the people I have around me. I think I have quite good instincts when it comes to people.

I've made friends since I've become better known, but I've never had anyone that's tried to take advantage or wanted to hang out with me just because of what I do. At least, I don't *think* so. It's never really crossed my mind.

A lot of the time, I end up meeting people who are in the music business, and I've stayed friends with a lot of producers and other singers. I think it's very normal to form friendships with people who are in the same industry as you, because you have a lot in common. My band are very good friends of mine because we're together so much and we've travelled all over the world. It's essential that you enjoy the company of the people you work closely with.

The people I'm closest to are still my family and the friends I grew up with. I've had the same close friends for years and years. My old school friend Diane and I still catch up on the phone, and I'm still friends with some of the Dixies. We share a lot of happy memories.

*

After my record deal with CBS came to an end, I signed with a German record label called Hansa, who were a huge hit-making company. Germany is the second-biggest market in the world for music, and the albums I was making were very much for the European market. That's where my music was selling the best, so it made sense to focus my attention there.

I released the album *Bitterblue* in 1991, and it did well for me. I changed my sound a bit in the nineties because I was ready to try something new. It was a bit more bluesy, hence the title, but not what I would call a 'blues' album. I always knew I would go back to the rockier sound, though, because when I'm on stage, I prefer singing the bigger ballads. The album went gold and platinum in Germany, Switzerland and Austria, and double platinum in Norway. I was so in demand that I went off on tour again.

The songs really were out of this world. Nik Kershaw wrote a track for me called 'He's Got A Hold On Me', and songwriter Albert Hammond – who has written for pretty much everyone you've ever heard of, including Diana Ross and Aretha Franklin – wrote 'Save Me' for the album, with the amazing Diane Warren. Giorgio Moroder of *Flashdance* fame wrote and produced four songs on the album, and I also recorded a song he wrote for the soundtrack of a German film called *Metropolis*. It was a restoration version of the original 1927 movie, so it was a really interesting project.

We recorded the song in Spain, but the main thing I remember was the hotel we stayed in. I felt like there was a horrible presence in the room. I didn't want Robert to go out and leave me there, and I was even frightened to go in the shower. I felt like something bad had happened there.

Despite the strange feeling I had in the hotel, the experience of working with Giorgio was great. Later, Robert and I went to his house for dinner when we were in Los Angeles, and he had mannequins everywhere. It was very strange, but maybe that was a thing in the nineties?

We also went out to a very famous restaurant there that all the stars go to. My manager, David, was with us, and we were tucking into our food when all of a sudden, David started jumping up and down. We asked him what was wrong, and he said there was a cockroach in his jacket sleeve. Oh, the glamour!

*

One of the first artists I ever went to see was Frankie Miller, who came to Wales with his band. He had the most incredible voice. Incredible! He blew me away.

Years later, when I was working with Jim Steinman in New York, he asked me who I'd like to duet with, and I immediately said, 'Frankie Miller. He has the most beautiful voice, and I've never forgotten seeing him live and being so inspired by him.'

Of course, Jim being Jim, he knew Frankie Miller, and suggested that we record a song called 'Tears' together, which

Frankie had written. The next thing I knew, Frankie Miller had flown to New York, and we were in a studio together recording the song, which appeared on *Faster Than the Speed of Night*. A few years later, in 1992, we recorded a second duet called 'Save Your Love', which featured on my album *Angel Heart*.

It was so wonderful to work with Frankie again, but sadly, in 1994, he suffered a brain aneurysm. He was unconscious for five months, and when he woke up, he was unable to speak or sing. He's got an amazing girlfriend called Annette who takes great care of him, and he has worked so hard at rehabilitating himself. In 1998, I was part of a benefit concert for Frankie at the Queen's Hall in Edinburgh, alongside Jools Holland and Paul Carrack. The concert was filmed for the BBC and it was later turned into a documentary called *Frankie Miller: Stubborn Kinda Fella*, which was about him trying to recover from his terrible illness. He is the most incredible, resilient man you can meet.

*

Angel Heart was my second release with Hansa, and I was ready to get behind it and make sure it was a hit. As well as the duet with Frankie, I had a great mixture of songs on there, including one co-written by Mutt Lange, a phenomenal writer who has written for the likes of Bryan Adams and Def Leppard. Jerry Lynn Williams, who wrote for B. B. King and Eric Clapton, also wrote for me on that album. I knew that if I could get the word out and people listened to it, they would love it.

But I got scuppered by CBS. They heard I was releasing a

new album, so they decided to get ahead of the game. By that point, 'The Best', 'Save Up All Your Tears', 'Don't Turn Around' and 'To Love Somebody' had all been massive hits, and they owned the rights to the songs I had recorded when I was signed to them. So, what did they do? They released *The Best of Bonnie Tyler* at the same time as I released *Angel Heart* and backed it up with TV advertising.

That *Best of* album sold over 600,000 copies and went platinum. It really overshadowed my new album. Even now, when I release a new album, my old record company often releases another *Best of* to make more money out of me.

*

Silhouette in Red was the last album I released with Hansa. It came out in October 1993 and marked my final collaboration with German producer Dieter Bohlen, who I worked with on all three of my albums with Hansa. He first found fame in the eighties duo Modern Talking and went on to become a judge on shows like *Germany's Got Talent*. He was the character everyone loved to hate, so he had a pantomime villain style, but I got on with him, and we worked well together.

One of the tracks on the album, 'Before We Get Any Closer', was produced by one of my former managers, Ronnie Scott, while my brother co-wrote a song called 'You Won't See Me Cry'. I also did a cover of Joe Cocker's 'You Are So Beautiful' and, by complete coincidence, I bumped into Joe in a hotel shortly afterwards. We ended up having a drink together, and I told him I'd recorded his song. He loved it, thankfully.

Silhouette in Red did well, and it was certified gold in

Norway on pre-sales alone. It later went platinum in Norway and Germany. It was the first one of my albums not to come out on vinyl, which was a sign of the changing times, I guess.

After my deal with Hansa finished, I signed with EastWest Records in Europe, who were a part of the Warner Music Group. I also signed my first US record contract in years, with Atlantic.

My first album release with both record companies was *Free Spirit*. Believe it or not, I worked with Jim Steinman again, so it was like a follow-up to *Secret Dreams and Forbidden Fire*, only thirteen years later! It's like I went to sleep for thirteen years and woke up, and Jim was back!

I re-recorded two of Jim's biggest hits, Meat Loaf's 'Two Out of Three Ain't Bad' and Air Supply's 'Making Love Out of Nothing at All'. Incredibly, the latter features my mother, Elsie, singing opera. I had an old tape she had recorded with my nephew Christopher on piano years before. I played it to Jim, and he was so impressed that he sampled her voice. It was so beautiful to hear her on one of my songs. I once asked her to come up on stage and sing it with me when I was doing a gig in Swansea's Singleton Park. I look back now, and I wish that she had, and that camera phones had been invented. I would love to have footage of my mother and I singing on stage together more than anything. I knew deep down there was no way she would ever do it. She was so shy. When friends or family used to come over to our house and ask her to sing, she would have to face the wall so she couldn't see anyone watching her. There was no way she was going to get up in front of all those people. But at least I tried.

For *Free Spirit*, I also worked with David Foster, who is another legendary producer and songwriter who has collaborated with everyone from Chicago to Michael Bublé. The album included a cover of 'Bridge Over Troubled Water', which is nothing short of a masterpiece (the original, I mean – I'm not going to toot my own horn like that!). It was very intimidating, but David Foster assured me I could do it justice. He knew I was feeling wobbly about it, so he said, 'Look, Bonnie, I know you can sing this. It'll be perfect for you, and I'll do a fantastic production.' And, of course, he did. This is a man who's won sixteen Grammys, after all.

I felt I had to be very respectful of the lyrics because it's such a beautiful song. The gorgeous Lenny Kravitz appears on the song too, but because of some sort of contractual obligation with his record company, Virgin, he wasn't allowed to be credited. It's crazy how this mad industry works.

Sadly, Jim and David were too busy to work on the entire album, so I worked with six producers in all, with the others being Humberto Gatica, Andy Hill, Jeff Lynne and Christopher Neil. It was mainly recorded at The Hit Factory in New York and Compass Point Studios in The Bahamas, which wasn't a terrible place to hang out!

I remember having a conversation with David Aspden, my then manager, at the time. He said, 'I really hope this album is going to take off,' and I replied, 'Listen, Dave, it's all happening now. Let's appreciate the now and not worry about what's going to happen.' So many people go through life worrying about the future and fretting about the past and missing the present moment. I'm someone who's always done the opposite: I stay rooted in the now, and I think that helps me to stay positive, even if things don't always work out how you would like them to.

CHAPTER SEVEN

If You Were a Woman

I kicked off the millennium in style by attending a superstar wedding, no less! Catherine Zeta-Jones is Robert's second cousin. Her father, David, is Robert's cousin, and her mother and father used to come to our Christmas parties every year. One year, Catherine brought Michael Douglas along for some mulled wine and a singalong! Catherine never acts starry and Michael was lovely and relaxed. He chatted to everyone like he was one of the neighbours and he seemed to have a lovely time.

What we didn't know at the time was that they were planning to get married soon, but before long, a very chic invite arrived for Robert and me, and the next time I saw Catherine, she said, 'Gaynor, I would love you to sing at the wedding, but if you'd rather not, I understand. I want you to enjoy yourself.'

How could I say no to that?

The wedding took place in the Plaza Hotel in New York. I am dreadful with red-carpet events; I knew there would be paps everywhere, so I was very nervous. I wasn't nervous about singing in front of everyone, because that's something I'm used to, but I've always avoided red carpets as much as possible. You'd be hard-pushed to find many photos of me at premieres and parties over the years, because I only went to something if I had to. Standing in front of a bank of photographers with a fixed grin on my face is not my idea of fun.

To try and avoid this, Robert and I came up with a clever plan. We booked ourselves into the Plaza so we could just walk downstairs to the wedding without having to do any of the red-carpet business. I was so relieved – but our plan was slightly foiled. A couple of nights before the wedding, Catherine and Michael had a get-together celebration at the glamorous Russian Tea Room restaurant in Midtown, so there was no getting around the photographers. Thankfully, they were much more interested in the Hollywood elite than they were in me and Robert.

The wedding was incredible. Absolutely amazing. I've got a lovely photo of me and Catherine, and I treasure it. Not because she's a big-name actress or anything, but because it brings back such great memories of the day.

I only ever allow myself one drink before I perform, and then I make up for it afterwards. I was sitting next to Mick Hucknall and we were having a great chat, but I was devastated because they were serving this amazing vintage champagne. I remember saying to him I was so upset because I was only allowed to sip one glass of it while everyone else was getting theirs topped up – and by the time I'd finished singing, it was all gone! But it was so worth it, because I loved getting to perform for them. I sang 'Total Eclipse of the Heart' and 'It's a Heartache', and I loved every second of it. I was wearing this long black gown with a split up the side, and I remember Mick saying to me, 'You've got great pins!' He sang as well, and my god, his voice live is something else.

Not surprisingly, it was a very star-studded affair. *Everybody* was there. Jack Nicholson, Goldie Hawn, Whoopie Goldberg, Danny DeVito and his lovely wife, Rhea Perlman, and Sir Anthony Hopkins (no relation, although I'm sure everyone in Wales *is* related somehow!). Everywhere you looked, there were film stars.

The only thing that spoiled it for Catherine was that one of the guests or staff took a picture and leaked it to one of the big magazines. It was supposed to be confidential until she was ready to share everything, so it was a very unkind thing to do. And to think it could have been someone she trusted too.

*

Everyone at Catherine's wedding was so gorgeous and glamorous. There is a lot of pressure in the entertainment industry to stay looking young and glam, and that's part of why I always have my hair and make-up done, even if I'm not going anywhere. I like to look presentable. I've also been very open about the fact I've had Botox. Thank goodness for Botox!

I tell everyone I have it, and I've been doing it for donkey's years. The very last time I had it, though, my eyebrows raised up, so I'm not sure whether I'm going to carry on having my forehead done, but I'll still have the crow's feet treated as and when necessary! I think too much was put in, and I looked a bit shocked all the time, so I was glad when it wore off. I've had a bit of Restylane filler in my laugh lines at times, but my general rule is to never have it lower than your crow's feet.

I'm sure people think I have Botox around my mouth, but that's not something I've ever done. If I'd had Botox there, I wouldn't be able to sing or blow out a candle!

173

I did hear a rumour that I've had a boob job, but I honestly haven't! In fact, I wish they were smaller than they are, I can tell you! I used to be quite flat-chested when I was young, and when I got married, I only had a thirty-two-inch bust. After the menopause, your body changes so much, and you don't feel like you have any control over it. I was very lucky that I didn't encounter all the terrible symptoms you hear about, like hot flashes and night sweats. Mine was relatively easy. My sisters were the same. I remember asking my mother about menopause when I was younger, and she said, 'Don't worry, you'll sail through it!' and she was right. The only thing that changed was my weight.

Getting older bloody sucks, when it comes to weight, because it becomes trickier to get rid of the extra pounds. But when I'm on stage, I feel like I'm in my prime because the adrenaline takes over, and I love staying strong and fit, so hopefully I'll be here for some time to come!

*

Part of getting older is beginning to lose the people you love, and it's the hardest thing in the world. A couple of years ago, my lovely, handsome brother Lynn passed, and it was devastating. He was such a kind, gentle man, and a remarkable person.

One of the many special things about him was that he took after Mam Hopkins in that we always felt like he had healing abilities. Many, many years ago, our youngest brother, Paul, was in a terrible car accident, and ended up in hospital for a very long time. He was driving to work very early in the morning and fell asleep at the wheel. He went through the windscreen, and he was very badly injured with glass in both eyes.

Because my mother was in her seventies by then, the hospital called me instead of her, and the panic I felt ... I don't even know how to describe it. That phone call and the drive to the hospital were two of the worst things that I've ever experienced.

When we arrived at the hospital, we could hear Paul screaming in pain, and I don't think I'll ever get that sound out of my head. We did everything we could to help him. We'd take soft pillows and tapes of his favourite shows for him to listen to. His girlfriend, Teresa, did everything for him, but she didn't mollycoddle him. She was determined that he would be able to do things for himself so she gave him a bit of a kick up the backside if he needed it. She was amazing for him, and she still is.

Paul was blinded in the accident, and for about six months, we thought he was going to be blind for life. The doctors did loads of tests on his eyes to try and determine if he would ever be able to see again. They did scans and then brought in a team of experts to give their opinion, and they all said they didn't think he would ever get his sight back. At one point my mother and I were called into a room by the matron and told that Paul would have to learn Braille to help him get through the rest of his life.

Lynn spent a lot of time with Paul over those six months, and although the doctors were insistent he was blinded for life, he recovered his sight. Even the doctors in the hospital called it a miracle. To this day, no one understands how Paul got his sight back. I'm not claiming that Lynn cured him, but I do like to keep an open mind about these kinds of things. There is so much more to life than we know about.

Lynn died in his sleep, and it was a big shock to all of us because he seemed fine. He had been to the hospital the day before because he thought there was something wrong with his heart. This was during the Covid pandemic, and although it was during one of the lockdown breaks, he had to go on his own. He stayed for eight hours while they did all sorts of tests on him, and then they said he was suffering from a hiatus hernia and sent him home.

That night he went to sleep, and he didn't wake up. I guess it's a nice way to go, because he didn't suffer, but we couldn't understand it. Nothing showed up on any of the tests he had, but maybe something was missed?

Robert woke me up at about 6am, and he said, 'Gaynor, Lynn has passed.'

I wouldn't accept it because it was such a shock. Robert and I went straight to his house. As I saw him lying on the bed, it finally began to sink in. I lay next to him and said goodbye. His eyes were ever so slightly open, and I could have sworn he was looking at me. Avis said the same thing.

He had a wonderful life. He adored his kids and grandkids, and he just wasn't ready to go. Lynn and his wife would have celebrated their diamond wedding anniversary earlier this year, but it wasn't to be. His lovely wife, Margaret, and their kids had a get-together on their anniversary anyway, and I'm sure his presence was felt.

*

Paul recovered well from his accident. He is sixty now, and he and Teresa are married with two boys, Andrew and James. Paul was, and is still, in a band called Sunshine Cab Co, and he's got the most fantastic rock voice.

I've never had a time when I wanted to step back from my career and take a break, because I feel very at home with what I do, but like all musical artists, I've had my ups and downs. The early nineties were a quiet time for me, but it's funny how things work out for the best because that quiet period turned out to be the perfect opportunity for me to spend time with my nephews.

Paul often had gigs on Fridays or Saturdays, so Andrew and James would stay with me and Robert most weekends, which was so lovely. It started off as a bit of babysitting here and there, but we loved it so much it turned into a regular thing. They would come on Friday evening, and we'd spend the weekend going to the beach to skim stones, to the boating lake or just hanging out at the house playing games, and then we'd take them home on a Sunday.

Andrew came first, and when James was old enough, he started coming too. When Andrew was about five, he came to stay with us in our old house while we were having the new house refurbished. One afternoon, we took him to the new house to see how things were coming along. Everything was in a state of disrepair, and it needed new bathrooms and floors. After a while, he said, 'Auntie Gaynor, I need to go to the toilet.' I told him, 'Auntie Gaynor hasn't got a toilet at the moment, so I'll take you to the bungalow in the grounds.' But it must have played on his mind for ages, because months later, his father took him to see Santa. When Santa asked

Andrew what he wanted for Christmas, he replied, 'Well, I had better ask for a toilet for my Auntie Gaynor, because she hasn't got one.' Paul said he nearly died of embarrassment. I thought it was so sweet of him – he could have asked for a toy, but no! He asked for a toilet for Auntie Gaynor . . .

The funny thing is, I still measure all the younger nephews and nieces to this day, just like I did when they were toddlers. I take them up to the attic and mark on the door frame how tall they all are. Some of them are teenagers now and are taller than the doorframes, but they still let me do it! They'll always be my little ones even though lots of them are grown up now.

Getting to spend so much time with Andrew and James was wonderful. We got very close to them, and it was like having kids of our own. When Robert and I first got married, I was enjoying singing in the clubs, and we had a good life, so we decided we'd put off having kids for the time being. Then the next year came and the next year came, and in the meantime, my career took off. I was so busy travelling and there was always something new happening. I love kids, and I adore my nieces and nephews, but I didn't have this strong urge to take a break from my career to have my own. If I'm being honest, I didn't think my career would last that long so I thought it would happen at some point, but I was always so busy. There didn't seem to be an obvious moment to say, 'Right, I'm ready. Now's the time!' I didn't ever dream about having a big family like I had growing up. It wasn't something I longed for.

Then, when I was thirty-nine, it suddenly *did* feel like the right time. We had just bought our new house, and we were feeling settled, and it felt like the right time to start a family. I know I was getting on a bit, but my mother had Paul when she was forty-three. Robert and I decided that we'd stop all precautions and see what happened. So, I came off the pill, and it was hardly any time at all before I found out I was pregnant. I felt disbelief at first, especially because the baby was due to come on Christmas Day. I was so excited I told quite a few people just before I got to the three-month mark, but looking back, maybe I should have waited, because you never know what's going to happen, do you?

One day, a few months into the pregnancy, I started bleeding. I phoned my sister Marlene, and I said, 'I'm spotting a bit. What should I do?' She told me to call the doctor and then sit quietly and relax as much as I could, but you can't help panicking in that situation.

When the doctor arrived he said to me, 'Look, I could tell you to rest up, but I'm a great believer in nature doing its own work.' So I knew I had already miscarried. I felt utterly numb.

Robert and I were both incredibly sad because it was a devastating thing to go through. We spoke to each other about it, and we comforted each other, but we knew that for whatever reason, it wasn't meant to be. My family were so kind and supportive, but I think I did whatever I could do *not* to think about it. I always had a funny feeling it was a boy, though. I don't know why. I just always had that sense.

I threw myself right into my work. In fact, crazily, I think I was working in Paris the following weekend. I told myself, *This is God's way of showing me I can have children, but it's not meant for me.* That helped me to make peace with it. The strange thing is, when I was growing up, I didn't ever feel that maternal, and I think it was a blessing to know that I could have children,

I wrote down all my feelings in a journal, and I cried and I got everything out. Then I put it away in the back of a cupboard with all my work diaries, and I haven't looked for it since. I mean, you have no choice but to get over it, do you? Otherwise it's too easy to wonder if you did something wrong. I wondered if being on flights didn't help, because I'd been travelling for work before I even knew I was pregnant.

I don't dwell on things that can't be changed, and I never have. I felt blessed that I knew I could get pregnant, because I did wonder if I would be like my Auntie Audrey who was never able to have children. I was lucky that I was able to get pregnant, but for whatever reason, the pregnancy didn't last for us.

*

In 1997, I recorded my album *All in One Voice* in Dublin, which is a place I never tire of visiting. The only problem is, you work hard and play hard over there, because it's so much fun. We were staying at the Clarence Hotel, right in the centre of everything, so it was too tempting not to go out for drinks or dinner.

I also recorded some of the album in Germany, and I worked with a fantastic Swedish songwriter called Per Andreasson. Of all my later albums, *All in One Voice* is probably the furthest removed from that rockier sound. It was softer and had some Celtic elements. Máire Brennan from

Clannad wrote a song for me with Denis Woods called 'We Can Start Here', and she also sang on it.

Incredibly, while I was working on that album, I was asked to do a duet with Andrea Bocelli on a beautiful song called 'Vivo Per Lei'. He had already done his vocals, so I put mine down too, and we sounded absolutely wonderful together. But I was signed to the record label Warner Brothers in Germany at that time, and they decided that they wanted a better deal than they had negotiated when Sarah Brightman did a duet with Andrea Bocelli the year before, which had gone to number one. Warner wanted more points, which is effectively a bigger percentage, but Andrea's record label, Sugar, pushed back. I said they could take *my* points as long as I got to put the song on the album, but Warner kept pushing and pushing for a better deal. In the end, I missed out on it completely, and I couldn't believe how they acted. Andrea ended up re-recording the song with a French artist, and it went straight to number one. I've missed out on quite a few things like that over the years, all thanks to certain record companies' stupidity.

That's why I decided to take back control with my next record. I went left field for my next album, *Heart Strings*. EMI Records had asked me to put together a collection of classic rock songs backed by a full-piece orchestra. I recorded it with the immense City of Prague Philharmonic Orchestra and my band. David Aspden and I chose thirteen songs for the album. For some reason, I picked tracks that had mainly been performed by male artists, like Roy Orbison, the Beatles and Phil Collins. It wasn't a deliberate choice; they were just all acts I have tremendous respect for. I also covered REM's massive hit, 'Everybody Hurts', which brought tears to my eyes.

I started by recording my vocals with just an acoustic guitar, and the orchestra parts were recorded over a week at the Smecky Music Studios and Barrandov Studios in Prague. I did some more vocals back in the UK, and then it was all pulled together by my manager, David, and my guitarist, Matt Prior. It was released in Scandinavia in October 2002 by a Danish record label called CMC, and then it was released around the rest of Europe the following March.

Just when you thought things couldn't get any stranger, I started working on my fourteenth album, *Simply Believe*. While I was in the process of getting the songs together, a French producer got in touch asking me if I would be interested in recording a bilingual version of 'Total Eclipse' with a French singer called Kareen Antonn. I was a bit sceptical, but when he sent me a demo, I got it. Before you can say, 'I'll have a croissant and red wine, please,' I was on a flight to Paris and in the studio with Kareen. We also recorded 'It's a Heartache' in the same style. The funny thing is, I can't speak French apart from the odd word, so I had to sing it phonetically.

I was planning to wait until my album was ready to come out before I released any of the songs as a single, but the promo version of '*Si Demain* (Turn Around)' was already being played at the radio stations and the demand was so strong that we decided to release it early on 22 December 2003. It stayed at number one for twelve weeks, and it was the fourth best-selling single of 2004 in all the French territories.

Simply Believe followed in April, and then we released our version of 'It's a Heartache', '*Si tout s'arrête*', that June. The single did well, going in at number twelve in France, but it didn't achieve anywhere near the number of sales '*Si Demain*' got. For some reason, that was the one to hit the spot.

*

What with one thing and another, it's safe to say that 'Total Eclipse' has always been a big part of my life. I don't even know how many times it's been covered or remixed. People often tell me that they hear dance versions of it. I know about Nicki French's 1995 dance version because that became a big hit, and I was surprised it took someone twelve years to do it. It wasn't my cup of tea because I wasn't really into dance music and I wasn't sure her voice was strong enough for it, but maybe you're more critical when you care about something that much. As I said back then when I was asked (many, many times!): good luck to her. She had a big hit record, and that's not an easy thing to do.

When karaoke first became a big thing, 'Total Eclipse of the Heart' was the number-one karaoke song in the UK. Sony sent me a karaoke machine to celebrate, and I gave it to my nieces, who loved it. I know it's still very popular at karaoke even now. I think it's one of those songs that everyone likes to belt out after they've had a few drinks, and because it's so well-known, other people can sing along. It amazes me how young some of the people are who like it. You would think they would see it as really old-fashioned, but it often pops up in films and TV shows, so I think that's how it gains new audiences.

It's the same with 'Holding Out for a Hero'. People often tell me they've been working out to that song. I've been told so many times over the years that as soon as people hear the intros to both 'Hero' and 'Total Eclipse', they know straight away what song it's going to be, and I think the fact that they're so instantly recognisable is a testament to Jim's brilliance.

Maybe they'll be the kind of songs that are around forever. I would like to think so. Jim Steinman was such an amazing man, so it would be a fitting tribute to him if his songs were played for decades to come. He wrote some of the best songs I've ever heard in my life, and it was a privilege to watch him work. Some people have a God-given talent, and he was one of them. Watching him was like watching a magician at work. He knew how to make anything sound incredible.

*

My album *Wings* came out in 2005, and it was the last one I worked on for eight years. I had worked relentlessly since I was seventeen, and I needed a break. Not a complete break from music, but from putting out albums and having to tour and promote them.

The highlights of making *Wings*, which was known as *Celebrate* in the UK, were the fact I got to record it mainly in Paris, I did some great re-recordings of 'It's a Heartache' and 'Total Eclipse', and my wonderful friend Lorraine Crosby provided guest vocals on 'I'll Stand By You' – and she got a credit this time!

I've been blessed with my career, and I wouldn't change a thing. It has been up and down at times, and I've gone with it. When I had a bit of a lean time, I enjoyed having that space. I loved going for long walks, and I had time to be Gaynor for a while and work out what I wanted to do next.

When I released 'Total Eclipse of the Heart' back in 1983, it was such a hard record to follow that the tracks I was releasing afterwards weren't really up to the same. But that was because it was a one-in-a-million song. 'Holding Out for a Hero' is the same. How can you have a number-one album in America and the UK at the same time and *not* think you've had some success in your career? If the hits that come afterwards aren't as big, it doesn't mean you've failed, and those achievements don't mean as much.

It didn't have a big emotional impact on me when I had down times. I wasn't crying myself to sleep because things were quieter. Heaven forbid! I realise it can have a massive effect on some people – being up one minute and down the next – but it didn't bother me at all. I didn't suddenly feel like a failure or as if I'd fallen out of fashion. And even if I had, who cares? It doesn't define who I am. I've always known who I am inside, and it would take a lot more than a dip in sales to make me feel as if I wasn't good enough. And what does 'good enough' really mean? Good enough for what or who? Even if I had never had a hit single and I'd played in the clubs all my life, I would still have been *good enough*. My mother drummed that into us from a young age. No matter what we did with our lives and no matter what went wrong, we would always be enough. I am so grateful for how well she taught us to be our true selves.

People think I've had these big gaps in my career, but I've always kept working, one way or another. I'm always working on ideas, speaking to producers, doing shows or planning my next album, so even when I say I'm taking a break, I don't take a *proper* one.

I would imagine from the outside, it looks like things aren't happening for me during these times, but that's rarely the case. For instance, although there was a period when things were quiet in the UK, I was still having triple-platinum-selling albums around Europe. I was selling 7,000 CDs a day in Germany. I sold 115,000 copies of *Bitterblue* in six weeks in Norway – and knocked Michael Jackson off the top of the charts.

I have great fans, especially in Germany. They've always supported me over there, and I've toured all over, time and time again. My German fans are very loyal, and they're right across the board. A lot of people were brought up on my music because they've heard it via their parents, and then they've played it to their own kids, so there's a very wide age range at my concerts.

Germany and Norway have always been two of my biggest markets. There was a time when I was the best-selling artist in Norway, but it is a small country! There used to be four million people living there, but now I think it's around five million. It's such a beautiful place, and when I fly over the country, I think, *They've probably got one of my albums in that house and that house and that house!*

Norway even gave me an award, which they call 'A Friend of Norway', and I visited twelve times in one year to perform and do signings. On one of these visits, I went to a four-storey shopping centre called Arken in Bergen, and the queues went from the top floor, where I was doing the signing, all the way to the bottom floor. These fans are nothing if not dedicated!

*

In 2012, I felt ready to get back into the studio. By that time, my partnership with David Aspden had come to a natural end, and a guy called Matt Davis became my manager. Matt had already been working with me since 1988 – initially as my tour manager – when I first decided to tour to support the 'Hide Your Heart' album release.

Matt, Robert and I went to Nashville, and we visited publishers looking for songs. I really wanted to try my hand at singing country songs, which I know sounds ironic considering how desperate I was to escape that sound in the seventies. But I meant *real* country rock, not just pretty, floaty songs like I sang back at the beginning of my career.

I like all kinds of music, and although I will always love rock, I do also like country and I love the blues. A lot of people ask why I haven't recorded a real blues album. If I have the time, I think I would like to at some point, but it's not on the cards at the moment. There are so many people I would love to work with if I had a chance, because I've always had such eclectic music tastes.

I've always been a big fan of Guns N' Roses, especially 'Sweet Child O' Mine'. Axl Rose was so sexy back then, and it's such a good track. Slash's guitar playing on that is unbelievable. *Appetite for Destruction* is a brilliant album from start to finish.

I still like all the rockers, like Bruce Springsteen and Bryan Adams. I think the Stereophonics are brilliant, and Tom Jones has still got it. There are also a lot of eighties acts that are still going strong and are brilliant. I quite often get asked if I'd like to be a part of one of those eighties revival tours that are very popular, but it's not for me. I prefer doing gigs on my own, although I imagine they must be a lot of fun.

I also love what Miley Cyrus does because she is one hundred per cent herself. I'm not just saying that because she did a cover of 'It's A Heartache' on YouTube, either. Liam and David, who run my Twitter account, sent her a message from me to say how much I loved the way that she performed it. She messaged back and said, 'Oh my god, there's no one girl that I listen to more than you, Bonnie.' What a great compliment. So of course I would love to duet with her – and also Rag'n'Bone Man. I love the tone of his voice, and I think we could harmonise really well.

While we were in Nashville, Matt, Robert and I visited the famous Bluebird Cafe during a songwriters' evening, where songwriters sit around a table with a guitar and showcase their songs. There was so much amazing talent there, and I was blown away. Some of the songs on my album came about as a result of that night.

I have dipped my toe into songwriting over the years, but I've never been really happy with what I've written. It was something I worried about for a while, but then I thought, *Lots of artists don't write songs, or they have co-writers who do a lot of it for them.* Tina Turner didn't write her own songs apart from 'Nutbush City Limits', although that is a fantastic song. I've written some songs with my brother Paul over the years, but I've never had hits with any of them, although Paul has had some great success.

I once wrote some songs with another Welsh singer called Gary Pickford-Hopkins, who worked with Rick Wakeman a lot. We co-wrote four songs for his album *GPH*, which was released in 2003. I also duetted with him on a track we co-wrote called 'Loving You Means Leaving You' for that album. Gary was a wonderful blues singer. But songwriting has never really been my forte. I'll leave it to the pros!

Jim Steinman was keen to get involved with my Nashville album, but sadly he wasn't able to due to poor health. Instead, I worked with a producer called David Huff, who instantly got the kind of record I was trying to make. I felt like I was in safe hands. We got a great selection of songs together, including two written by Desmond Child, and I also covered a couple of tracks that I love: 'Flat on the Floor', which was originally on Carrie Underwood's 2007 album *Carnival Ride*, and 'All I Ever Wanted', a cracking song that was first recorded by Beau Davidson in 2010. The result was my 2013 album, *Rocks and Honey*.

*

When someone from the BBC heard *Rocks and Honey*, they loved the track 'Believe in Me', which was one of the ones Desmond Child had written for me. They asked me if I would represent the UK at the Eurovision Song Contest singing that song. I was shocked when they asked me, because when they first approached me to do it back in 1983, I just said 'No'. At the time I was at number one in the UK and US album charts, and it just didn't feel right to say yes because I was already enjoying so much success. I noticed that their radio stations stopped playing my records as much after that, but I have no idea if it was as a direct result of me turning them down.

Now, though, I knew Eurovision would be great publicity for my new album, so I thought, *Why not?* It's a great vehicle for promotion, and I knew I would probably sell a lot of concert tickets off the back of it.

Even when I agreed to take part, I knew I had no chance of winning. It was still so political back then, with all the neighbouring countries voting for each other. The UK had always been way down on the popularity list. No other countries seemed to like us, apart from Ireland. But that didn't matter – I was there for the experience.

The contest was held in Malmö in Sweden. The atmosphere was amazing, and people all over Wales were having parties and egging me on, which was brilliant. I was unbelievably nervous about it. I was a well-established artist, and everybody else was just starting out – it felt a bit strange. But when I walked behind that British flag in the arena, the roar from the crowd was amazing. I thought the roof was going to come off! The support that I got was incredible.

When you're up on that stage, you can't let yourself think about how many millions of people are watching the show, or you'd just freeze! I had to stop my mind from going there. Something crazy like over 120 million people tune in every year. You've got to focus on the crowd in front of you and imagine you're just singing for them.

I ended up coming nineteenth in the competition, which wasn't my finest moment, but you can't win at everything – and if you don't try, you'll never know.

I didn't come away empty-handed, though. After the show, I was given two Eurovision Song Contest Radio Awards for Best Song and Best Singer, which were voted for by the fans, followers and listeners. I was the first UK representative ever to be given one, so to get two was wonderful. The song also scored the highest Eurovision-related new entry on that week's Top 100 UK Singles Chart, so it can't have been all bad!

Eurovision is such a mammoth production, and people love it so much. As soon as the winning country is announced, all the superfans are on their phones booking hotels for the following year. I thought our entrant for 2023, Mae Muller, was great, and I really liked her song. It seems unfair that she didn't do better. You just never know with Eurovision, but I do think we deserve to score more highly than we often do.

I was a big fan of Mae, as I am of many other female artists. I am extremely supportive of women in music, and I always have been. The music business has shifted a lot since I started out, but I didn't ever feel like it was more difficult for me to be taken seriously because I was female. Maybe it was because I'd been working from such a young age. It didn't even cross my mind that I would be discriminated against or given fewer opportunities than male singers. I can rock with the best of them!

I can say the same for most of the female singers that are around at the moment. There's so much strength and passion, and this generation are showing just how powerful women can be. There would be times in my early career when I would play festivals or gigs and be the only woman on the line-up, but that has changed a lot. Not enough, but a lot.

I was blessed that I still had some incredible female role models to look up to. Janis Joplin showed me so much about what it means to sing with soul, and in such a beautiful way.

The emotion she could draw from a single word was astounding. And watching Tina Turner forge this incredibly successful solo career after all she'd been through with Ike . . . It takes a real fighter to get up and try again like that, and her talent radiated from her beautiful face.

Young girls and women wanting to be an artist now have got so many role models to choose from. I mean, look at the likes of Beyoncé, Miley Cyrus, Adele, Pink and Emeli Sandé. They're very different, but they're all bloody brilliant. You know just from looking at them that there's no way they're letting a group of men pull the strings behind the scenes. They are independent, they know what they want and they're grabbing it with both hands. If that isn't inspirational, what is?

Desmond Child wrote a fantastic song for my album *The Best is Yet to Come* called 'Stronger than a Man'. There's a line that's always stuck with me: 'A woman's place is anywhere a woman wants to stand.'

What a powerful message. We still have a long way to go in terms of equality and female representation, but we are pushing through. I loved this TikTok post that was part of the #WeAreHere campaign that was launched as part of International Women's Day in 2021:

Where are all the women? 22% of chart music artists are women. 2% of music producers are female, and only 0.5% of producers are women of colour. 2% of classical works performed at concerts were written by women, and 1 in 103 orchestra trumpet players are women. This International Women's Day, we are calling out the lack of attention, visibility, acknowledgements and freedom the world gives women. So, next time you ask 'Where are the women in music?', #WeAreHere.

*

I could talk all day about all the performances I've loved. I've been lucky enough to perform all around the world and go to amazing awards shows like the BRITs and the Grammys.

One of my most memorable performances was when Royal Caribbean marked the eclipse in 2017 by getting me to perform 'Total Eclipse' on the deck of the cruise ship *Oasis of the Seas*, alongside the rock band DNCE. Joe Jonas from the Jonas Brothers is a member of the group, and he's lovely.

It was so packed, and the atmosphere was electric; it was mega. It was lovely to work with such a cool, gorgeous band, and they did a fantastic version of my song. Joe's voice is amazing, which isn't that surprising considering he's a megastar!

I gained another number-one single that summer when 'Total Eclipse' became the most downloaded song during the eclipse. There was a 214 per cent increase in Spotify streams in the UK alone, and a 500 per cent increase in global digital sales! I guess you can't get a song that ties in better!

I never get bored of singing my hits. People assume I must be sick to death of 'Total Eclipse', but it's one of those songs I don't think you can ever get bored of. I'm not one for singing it around the house, though. I don't sing anything around the house, not even in the bath or shower. I'm usually too busy listening to demos for my new album and trying to learn the lyrics in my head.

I love the reaction from the crowd when the intro to 'Total Eclipse' kicks in. I get such an uplift from seeing people happy, and the song feels a bit different every time I perform it.

I've got a pre-stage ritual I do before gigs, but it's nothing complicated. These days, I often phone my voice coach and have a session with him. He's called James Windsor, and he's made such a difference to my voice over the years. I ring him about two or three times a week, and I even did it during lockdown to keep my voice in shape. He's done me the power of good. I don't get a chance to go and see him often because he's based in London, but the phone sessions work brilliantly.

Once I've spoken to him, I'll have one shot of Jack Daniel's and a Red Bull to give me a bit of a kick and some energy. Red Bull really does give me wings. Then I get together with the boys in the band, and we all put our hands on top of each other's and lift them in the air, and bellow out a good 'Whoop!' Then it's showtime.

When we come off stage, the band, crew and I may have another drink or two together, but there's no wild partying! I've never been a diva when it comes to having a rider, but I do always ask for some wine, Diet Coke, water and Jack Daniel's for me *and* the boys, plus a few snacks for people to share. I've heard horror stories about some people's riders, which I won't repeat, but I've always been easygoing about mine. One thing I do like is comfy seating, but I don't care what colour the walls in the dressing room are! Some of the rock places I perform in are proper dives, so I can't imagine what they would say if I asked for the walls to be painted pink and a leopard-print chaise longue to be shipped in. I do want a lighted mirror to be able to do my make-up in, and a full-length mirror, but that's the norm!

But for me, it's all about the performance. What's going on out front is far more important than what's going on in the back. I do often invite some of the fans back to the dressing room after a show for a drink, though. One fan has been to see me 168 times. Yep – 168 shows! There are quite a few fans that have been around for a long time, so I know them well, and that's lovely. When you're away from home for a while, it's nice to see a friendly face you haven't seen in ages and have a catch-up.

I've had a few mishaps on stage over the years, but with the number of gigs I've done, I guess that's to be expected. My funniest one was right back in the day when I was still a Dixie. Wigs were very fashionable at the time, and I had a short Mia Farrow-style wig that I loved. She had just got married to Frank Sinatra, and everyone was talking about how cool she looked with her short hair. I didn't want to cut my own, so I got this wig that was the double of her hairstyle.

The first time I wore it, I flattened my own hair down and fastened it with clips so it was as close to my head as possible. I popped on the wig, but as I was walking out on stage, I tripped over a wire and my wig came flying off. I was so embarrassed. A load of the Swansea football team were in that night, and they all saw. I let out a little scream and ran backstage to reattach it.

I don't experience that feeling of *Oh no, another airport*, or *Argh, not another gig*, because I truly adore it. I have had times over my career where I've been rushing from one country to another, and I'm on and off planes, and I've lost track of where I am and what day it is. I've even had to ask someone which country we're in. It does get a bit confusing sometimes! I've said 'Thank you' in German a few times when I'm in France, or 'Welcome!' in Swedish, when I'm actually in Spain. America isn't really on my radar anymore, because I haven't had a hit over there since 'Holding Out for a Hero' in 1987, and I have so many other things going on.

Food is one of the most fascinating parts of all the travelling I've been lucky enough to do. I've tried so many different cuisines and eaten in some beautiful restaurants. The strangest thing I've ever eaten was when I was in Japan. We went for a meal at a restaurant that was supposed to be amazing. You chose your main meal, and then you got given these little bowls on the table as mystery side dishes. I tried what looked like braised beef in a broth, but it turned out to be lung. It was bloody awful! The foulest thing I've ever tasted. Another time I ate snake in Hong Kong, although I didn't realise what it was until after I'd swallowed it. I felt nauseous once I found out. It didn't taste that bad; I just would have appreciated a heads-up!

CHAPTER EIGHT

The Best Is Yet to Come

Do you remember how I mentioned earlier in the book Kevin Dunne, my former bandmate, came back into my life? Well, now is that time.

A few years after I'd released *Rocks and Honey*, I was back in Wales and Kevin got in touch to say he'd written some songs, and he would love me to listen to them. I was very confused, because as far as I knew, Kevin had never written a song in his life.

I was very upfront with him and said, 'I will listen to them, but I will tell you the absolute truth about them, because that's only fair. I won't tell you I like them if I don't; I won't string you along.'

He thought that was fair enough, so I had a listen. It sounds terrible, but I wasn't expecting much. As it turns out, though, I really liked some of them – they were fabulous. I rang him and said, 'Where have these come from? All of a sudden you come at me with these songs! Fuck, they're fantastic! I've got to try them as demos at the very least to see what we can do.'

We did some demos, and they sounded great. I was raring to go. Kevin said he had a contact in Nashville who wanted to produce them. The contact turned out to be Johnny Cash's son, John Carter Cash.

After a few calls, Robert, Kevin, Matt and I flew over to Nashville, and we recorded the tracks in a studio in the garden of Johnny Cash's former home, aptly named Cash Cabin.

For some reason, the songs just didn't work out. Kevin wasn't keen on the production, because he had a very set sound for them in his head, and he didn't feel like he had captured the *feel* of the songs. John has his own way of doing things, as all producers do, and there was a bit of a clash.

Kevin was disappointed, but he was still determined to get the songs into the hands of the right producer. He had someone else in mind, who turned out to be another huge blast from the past – David Mackay.

David and I had been in touch briefly in 2016 when he was putting together a tribute album called *Frankie Miller's Double Take*, to help raise money for Frankie. So many established artists covered Frankie's songs, including Rod Stewart, Elton John, Willie Nelson and Huey Lewis. I sang a song called 'True Love', which is a beautiful track. It was such a lovely thing for David to have done, but I didn't have a huge amount of contact with him during that process, so we hadn't seen each other properly for about forty years. He was the very first person who had produced me, and now it was like things were coming full circle again. Something about it felt right.

David did a brilliant job of knocking Kevin's songs into shape, and I think a part of that was down to how comfortable I felt with him. Things flowed so easily because we were used to working together. Granted, it had been several decades since the last time we'd been in a studio together, but it felt very natural, as if it was meant to be. David's got such a brilliant work ethic, and he's very well respected in the music industry. He's worked with anyone and everyone. I've been lucky enough to work with many wonderful producers in my time, like Jim Steinman and Desmond Child, but David is a very, very special guy.

We did all the recording in David's studio at his house in Surrey, and it ended up being one of the most enjoyable experiences I've ever had making an album. It was so lovely seeing his wife, Brenda, again too, and David, Robert and I hung out as if no time had passed. We all got on like a house on fire.

We got into a routine where David would start working on the tracks at around 6am – which is way, way too early for me – and then I would arrive at around midday, and we'd work through until around 5pm.

Robert and I stayed in a beautiful hotel up the road, and at 5pm, we could all down tools and open red wine or champagne, and we'd all have a few drinks. Then Brenda would cook a nice meal, or we'd go to a local restaurant. It was a really lovely way to make an album.

I did a duet with Francis Rossi for the album at his studio down the road from David's. The song was called 'Someone's Rockin' Your Heart', which Francis wrote with a guy called Robert Young. I've known Francis forever, and he's a cracking chap. He's so funny, we laughed all the way through the recording.

David is a huge tennis fan, and that year he happened to go to Wimbledon with Sir Barry Gibb. He told Barry he was working on my album, and he told me he'd asked Barry to write me a song. Of course, I thought he was kidding, and then a few months later, Barry sent David this stunning song called 'Seven Waves Away'. So it wasn't a joke after all. Things were getting better and better!

During a break in recording, Sir Cliff Richard – or Cliff, as he's known to me and Robert – invited us to go and stay at his wonderful home in Barbados. We had become friends after appearing on a local radio station together in Portugal, because he's got a villa there a stone's throw from ours. Quite often, we'd all go out on one of our boats or get together for lunch or dinner.

Barbados was absolute paradise, but it was quite strange waking up and looking out the window to see Cliff weeding his garden.

While Robert and I were in Barbados, the stars aligned, and I finally got the chance to do one of my dream duets. One afternoon, we went to lunch at a restaurant called Sandy Lane. It was hosted by a guy called Ricky, who is very good friends with Rod Stewart. I was chatting to Ricky, and I said, 'Oh my god, I would love to do a duet with Rod.' I'd been called 'the female Rod Stewart' countless times over the years, and I was so intrigued to see what our voices would sound like together.

Ricky told me to email him and said he would pass my message on to Rod. It took me a few months to send the email because I was waiting for the right song to come along, and it did thanks to Chris Norman from the band Smokie. Chris had written a song called 'Battle of the Sexes', and as soon as I heard it, I knew it would work well for me and Rod.

Originally, Chris wanted to sing it with me, but I asked if I could send it to Rod, and he agreed. Rod came back and said he would do it, and I was over the bloody moon. Frustratingly, though, our schedules completely clashed. When I was in London, he was in LA, and when he was in London, I was on tour. We ended up recording our vocals separately, but the most important thing to me was that after all those years of wanting to duet with Rod, it was in the bag.

I went back to Portugal, and I told Cliff all about the album over dinner. Cliff's known David Mackay forever, and he was very impressed that Barry had penned a song for me. I played Cliff some of the songs we'd already recorded, and he said, 'Well, why don't we do a duet together?' We waited for the right song to come along, and it did, in the form of an amazing track written by Steve Womack called 'Taking Control'.

Songwriter Amy Wadge, who co-wrote Ed Sheeran's 'Thinking Out Loud' and Sam Ryder's Eurovision song, 'Space Man', also wrote a beautiful song for me called 'Older'. Everything fell into place so naturally.

That album became *Between the Earth and the Stars*, which I released in February 2019. I wanted the album reveal to be a real event, so my digital team closed down my website on 22 January 2019 and wrote, 'Check back for an exciting announcement on 31 January 2019!'

They did a fabulous job at redesigning it, and on the 31st my new website burst back into life with a mini-documentary about the album that featured clips and teasers of some of the songs. I released the first single, 'Hold On', the following day.

The album was successful in the UK, if not huge, but it did really well in Germany and some other European countries. I went on an amazing tour between April and June where I covered twenty-three dates in France, Belgium, Germany, Switzerland, the Netherlands, Luxembourg and Austria. It's always exciting when you have new music to perform, and it was bloody fantastic.

David and I had such a great experience making the album we decided to start working on another one almost straight away. Because I'd had some amazing duets on *Between the Earth and the Stars*, we decided we'd strip this one right back and make it all about me and the mic. A lady called Miriam Stockley did all the backing vocals. I'd worked with her on *Between the Earth and the Stars* and my 1995 album, *Free Spirit*, and she is fabulous.

This album had what I would describe as a classic rock-pop sound, and I felt like I was going back to my roots a bit more. I've got more of the great Steve Womack's songs on there, including 'Call Me Thunder' and 'Stuck To My Guns'. Because I've worked with Steve in the past, he knows what kind of songs suit my voice, so I always feel like he gets me.

The ever-amazing Desmond Child wrote a song for me after I told him I wanted something 'really loud and ballsy!' He heard me loud and clear, and came up with one of my favourite tracks on the album, 'Stronger than a Man'.

I took a massive risk, covering one of my favourite songs of all time, 10cc's 'I'm Not In Love'. It's another one of those songs that you think should probably be left well alone, but I just couldn't help myself! It had been on my mind to try and do a version of it for years, and I went for it. I decided if it was terrible, we didn't have to include it, but it wasn't. Everyone David and I played it to loved it.

I called the album *The Best is Yet to Come* because it was released in February 2021, during the pandemic, and we all needed some positivity during that awful time. It was my first physical album to be released in America since *Free Spirit* in 1996, and it went to number nine in the UK album chart. I had planned to do a thirty-eight-date tour of Europe to promote the album, but that was postponed until 2023 due to Covid.

Shortly after I released *The Best is Yet to Come*, I heard the incredibly sad news that Jim Steinman had passed away from kidney failure. He died on 19 April 2021 in Connecticut, and I was in absolute shock when I heard. I felt like he was invincible. He was so unbelievably talented, but he didn't have the ego to go with it. I owe the rock era of my career to him and will be forever grateful. He was instrumental in building my career. He was amazing, crazy and one of a kind.

I had so much I wanted to say about him, and I worked on a tribute for hours, trying to find the right words. In the end, I wrote this, and it went up on my social media accounts. I just hope it's a fitting tribute to a wonderful, wonderful man.

I am absolutely devastated to learn of the passing of my long-term friend and musical mentor Jim Steinman.

Jim wrote and produced some of the most iconic rock songs of all time and I was massively privileged to have been given some of them by him. I made two albums with Jim, despite my record company initially thinking he wouldn't want to work with me. Thankfully, they were wrong, and I can say without any doubt that Jim was a true genius.

He was also a funny, kind, supportive and deeply caring human being and the world is a better place for his life and his work, and a worse one for his passing. I will always be grateful to him for the opportunity to work with him and also to know him.

Rest in peace Jim, my friend.

I like to think he's out there somewhere, listening to the music he loved so dearly.

*

Covid was such a strange and awful time for everyone. Who could have predicted that? I'd been working in Sweden, and I had a week off after my last show in March 2020. Robert suggested we spent the week in Portugal, and we ended up staying there for the whole two years, so we were incredibly grateful.

It was the first time I'd had a proper break from work since I was seventeen, apart from when I had my throat operation, so it felt very strange not to be planning ahead or packing and unpacking cases. It took me a while to get used to it, as it did everyone. It was like experiencing retirement, and it made me realise I am not ready for it.

Of course, we missed our families, but no one could see theirs, so we were in the same position as everyone else. There were a lot of Zoom catch-ups and phone calls, but we had it very easy compared to some people. Lots of people had to spend the lockdowns on their own, or they were stuck inside with people they didn't like, which must have been a nightmare. And all those people who weren't able to work ... So many touring musicians I know were panicking. They had gone from being booked up for months at a time to having no work at all, and a lot of them couldn't get help from the government. It was a horrendous time all round.

I spent a lot of time cleaning out cupboards and drawers, but I didn't do any of the live streams a lot of artists were doing from home. I would have felt ridiculous. I did do a few nice TV interviews, which broke up the boredom. Though I found myself having to do my own roots for the first time, which was very difficult!

I didn't quite pull off a successful banana bread, but I did cook a lot, and I finally learned to swim. My friend Sue, who was one of the Dixies, started teaching me before Covid. Then during lockdown, Robert helped me, and it all started to click into place. Once I got the hang of it, I thought, *This is so bloody easy. Why haven't I done it before?* Now I love it.

I did end up in hospital in Faro at one point during lockdown, which is not somewhere you want to be in the middle of a pandemic, but I felt so unwell I had no choice. I had terrible stomach pain, and the doctors thought I might have a blocked bowel.

I had to stay in to be assessed in case it was anything really serious, so they cut me all the way down the middle of my stomach to do an investigation. Amazingly, you can hardly see the scar now, but they didn't ever find out what was causing my symptoms.

My family were all very worried about me, but it happened near the end of lockdown, when they were just starting to allow people to fly again. My brother Paul was able to get on a plane to come and see me, but when he arrived at the hospital, they wouldn't let him in. I was gutted.

I still can't believe we lost Meat Loaf, potentially to Covid.

He died on 20 January 2022, and it was said that he was suffering from Covid before he passed, but to this day I don't know the truth of how he died. It was devastating for his family, friends and fans. He had been a part of my life for so long, and it came out of nowhere. I mean, it's Meat Loaf. How can someone that strong and powerful pass away so suddenly? He was a total legend and a wonderful person to work with. I don't think anyone had the same stage presence he had. I always used to be transfixed watching him.

It was a fantastically fitting tribute when I heard that his fans were buying all his old albums. He had something like eight new entries in the charts the week after he left us. I think that would have made him smile.

*

I celebrated forty years of 'Total Eclipse' in 2023, and it's unbelievable it's been that long. I got invited to go on *This Morning* to talk about the song and perform. The lovely thing about going on *This Morning* is that it's filmed in the same studios where they used to record *Top of the Pops*, and all the old memories came flooding back. When I went into the bar area, it reminded me of the old days when it was full of people in weird costumes who were filming dramas, and it was so buzzy. We'd all be drinking together, the actors and the pop stars having a glass of wine after filming.

Although it was so lovely to have a chat with Josie Gibson and Craig Doyle and celebrate the song, my 'live' performance that morning was a disaster.

I'd been invited on the show a few weeks before, but I'd

had to postpone it because of a diary clash. Even though I was very unwell in the days leading up to my rescheduled appearance and my doctor had diagnosed me with a virus, I didn't feel like I could postpone it again, so I went ahead.

I had planned to sing live because I always do. I never, ever mime (though there have been TV shows, often in Europe, who make you). But during rehearsals, it became really clear that there was no way I was going to sound good enough. It was way too late for me to pull out of singing because they had already talked about it and billed it as a live performance, so of course that's what people were expecting.

I was much more husky than usual in the interview, and Josie and Craig were so lovely, but when I was up at the mic and Josie announced that I was about to sing live, I thought, *Oh shit, no one's told Josie I'm not singing live now, and I haven't had a chance to mention it, so I'm just going to have to get on with it.* It was a nightmare because I knew I'd have to mime.

There was nothing for it but to mime, and I got such a battering from the public online. I'm not a big one for social media – I have two great guys called Liam and David who do it all for me, so I don't go on Twitter and Instagram very often – but even I knew there was a backlash. It was mortifying. All the keyboard warriors were having such a go at me that my manager had to put out a statement explaining what had happened:

Bonnie is incredibly disappointed that she had to lip-synch on ITV's *This Morning* today. However, she woke up with a terribly sore throat, which was obvious from her speaking voice during the interview, and at rehearsals it was clear she couldn't sing today. So rather than let TV and her fans down at the last moment, she decided to mime instead. In fact, I have just spoken to her on the phone and it's got a lot worse, she can hardly speak at all now.

Everyone should be assured that Bonnie's voice is still very strong when she doesn't have a cold, as anyone coming to any of her live shows this year will be able to hear for themselves.

She is very sorry if anyone felt let down by her having to mime, she actually hates miming and never usually does it, and is looking forward to her voice being back to its normal strength very soon.

I hope I get invited back on to the show at some point so I'm able to show the viewers that I really can sing just as well as I always have done!

My throat kept getting worse and worse, and I completely lost my voice for a month. That's the first time in my life that's happened. Even when I had the nodules on my vocal cords in the seventies I *could* still speak; I just wasn't allowed to. I had the most horrendous cough, too, and I took everything under the sun to get rid of it, but it refused to bugger off. I honestly wondered if I'd ever talk again at some points. I had a show to do in Portugal at the end of April, and I was so lucky because I got my voice back just in time. It's a nightmare for anyone to lose their voice, let alone when they've got shows to perform!

*

I'm pretty good at keeping up with technology, but I am glad I'm not glued to social media like some people are. I do enjoy looking at it, and I love having my accounts so I can keep my fans updated with what I'm doing. It's such a great promotional tool.

I'm very open about the fact I don't do all my own updates. The words and the pictures come from me, but Liam and David keep everything updated and message or call me when they want quotes or to do a catch-up. They're also great at posting old videos or interviews of me – and my goodness, they bring back memories.

I don't want to be one of those people who pretend they do everything themselves when they don't. I always credit the people who help me. I would never be able to keep the likes of Instagram and Twitter updated as well as Liam and David do. I don't have the time, and I know that if it was left up to me, I would probably forget to post anything.

Liam and David are also in charge of my website, so they let people know when I've got shows or appearances coming up and make sure my bio is up to date, as well as all the other things that I know I would let slide. I prefer to concentrate on my music and let someone who knows what they're doing take charge.

I do enjoy the streaming services, even if I'm not 100 per cent sure how it all works. I know it's not the same as going into a shop and buying records, but I love the idea of people across the world having instant access to my old and new songs. So far on Spotify, I've had over 195 million streams, over 35 million listeners from 183 countries, and nearly 14 million hours of my music has been listened to. I mean, can you believe that? It's mind-blowing when you think about it.

We had no idea how many people were listening to our

music before all these facts and figures were available. We knew how many records we sold and that told us a lot, but I like knowing the statistics. Especially as it's all easy to understand, even for me!

*

It's ironic that despite leaving school at sixteen, I now have two honorary degrees: one from Cardiff University and one from Swansea University. I'm officially a doctor now, but not the sort that could help out if there was an emergency on a plane!

Getting awarded my MBE in 2023 was, needless to say, one of the highlights of my life. I got the award for both my music and my charity work. I found out about it when I was sent a letter from the House of Commons asking me if I would accept an MBE. Of course I'd love to accept it. Just try and stop me!

I knew quite a few months beforehand that it was happening, but when I received a follow-up letter with the date of the ceremony, it felt much more real. It meant even more to me because our wonderful late Queen had included me in her final Birthday Honours List, which was so special. I was allowed to take three people with me, so needless to say Robert came, along with my sister Marlene and her husband, Gwyn. We travelled to Windsor Castle in our car, and we were all on cloud nine. It was a long day because a number of other people were being honoured, but it gave us a great opportunity to meet some amazing people and take in the magnificence of the castle.

When it was my turn to collect my award, we were taken

into the cloakroom area to hang up our coats, and then we were ushered into a beautiful room with marvellous paintings everywhere. It was glorious. I mean, you're walking through a castle, for goodness' sake. You can't help but be hugely impressed with how beautiful everything is.

We were shown into the room where the presentation was taking place, and Robert, Marlene and Gwyn were escorted to the other side of the room so they could watch the ceremony. I stood in a line, and when it was my turn to be presented, I was called up. We'd been shown how to do the bow properly, and I was hoping my knees wouldn't start wobbling or creaking, because I get terrible trouble with them.

Prince William presented me with my MBE, and that was so lovely because I'd met him the year before when I'd performed at a concert for our late Queen's Platinum Jubilee. I was nervous to meet him again that day, but I needn't have been because he was so kind.

After I'd done my little bow and taken a step back, he said to me, 'It's so lovely to see you again. I met you in Cardiff.' As if I'd forgotten that! He put me totally at ease and asked me who I was there with. Then he motioned over to my husband and sister and brother-in-law, and gave them a nice smile. They were all thrilled.

We had some lovely photos taken. You pay for those and the money goes towards the Prince's Trust, who I'm an ambassador for. I've done some work for them over the years, and I'm hoping to do more.

Funnily enough, my charity work wasn't mentioned during the ceremony, which is strange because it was the charities who wrote letters saying that they would like me to have some recognition. Not that I'm looking for recognition; that's absolutely not the reason I support the causes I do. I do it because I'm in an incredibly privileged position where I can support them, and because I want to.

I've supported a lot of different charities over the years, but my main ones are Cerebral Palsy Cymru near Cardiff, which is an incredible charity for children with cerebral palsy, and a wonderful children's hospital called Noah's Ark. They do amazing work and, as so many people in the public eye say, I have a platform, and it takes so little to help raise awareness for a charity, but it can make a big difference to them.

We all went out for a lovely lunch in Windsor after the ceremony, and then we stayed in a hotel, so we made a real day of it. I didn't wear my MBE out for lunch. I thought that might be a bit much. I kept it in my bag, but I didn't let my bag out of my sight all day. I wish my parents could have been with me that day. They would have been so proud of me.

*

I've met King Charles on several occasions, and he's always been so lovely to me. He seems genuinely interested in people, and he makes such an effort to put you at ease. I've met him through several charities, and he's always asking you lots of questions. I guess he gets asked questions himself so often it's probably nice for him to let someone else do the talking.

And doesn't he look so incredibly happy with Camilla? It's so wonderful to see. They make a great couple.

Don't get me wrong, I thought Diana was wonderful too, and such a beautiful woman. I was devastated when she died.

I was like a blithering idiot when I met her. She asked me where I was from, and I said, 'Skewen.' As if she'd bloody know where Skewen is! Why didn't I just say Swansea or Wales? I felt like such an idiot.

Back when he was still Prince Charles rather than the King, Charles came to Cardiff for the premiere of an animated film called *Final Fantasy: The Spirits Within*, and Robert and I were invited along. I only ended up sitting next to Prince Charles in the cinema, while the actress Nerys Hughes was on the other side of him. Robert was next to me, and I told Prince Charles that Robert was one of his escorts during his investiture at Caernarfon Castle in 1969. Prince Charles found that fascinating, so he and Robert chatted quite a lot.

I can't believe I'm going to admit this, but Charles's equerry once told me that the prince sometimes invited artists to the home he has in Wales to perform, and he gave me his card to arrange it – but I only went and bloody lost it. I was too embarrassed to phone up one of the palaces and try and explain what had happened in case they thought I was crazy!

I have a room at my house in Wales where I keep all my awards. It's also a music room, and there are a lot of gold discs on the walls. I know a lot of people don't keep their gold records, and I have given a lot away to charity over the years, but I've kept the ones that mean a lot to me.

Even though the room is quite bright when you're in there, it's very discreet. My house is quite big, and the awards are tucked back in the corner of the music room, so you wouldn't know they were there unless I showed you. No one is going to walk into the house and be confronted with a wall of discs.

That would be way too flashy for me. I prefer having photos of my family and friends around the place. They're far more important to me, and I love feeling like I'm surrounded by the people I love. Awards are a bit of a temporary high, and they can't hug you like someone you love can!

It's always nice to get an award, but it's not the reason I do what I do. I was given a gold disc for 'Total Eclipse of the Heart' and another one for *Faster Than the Speed of Night* at the same time. A very important gentleman called Maurice Oberstein, who was the most powerful record company chairman in Europe, presented them to me in front of the record company execs. His dog was there too. (He always had his dog with him; he was famous for it!) I got excited and gave a little speech where I said, 'I'm really pleased to get two more. I've got pontoon now; I've got twenty-one!' Everyone expected me to be very proper, but I was excited – and you can't take yourself too seriously, can you?

I've been lucky enough to meet some incredible people over the years, but Prince William and King Charles are very high on that list. Bryan Adams is a wonderful man, Jon Bon Jovi was great, and I loved meeting Alice Cooper because everyone assumes he's going to be scary, but he's such a nice man. He's very funny, and in his spare time, he helps to feed the homeless, which I think is marvellous. It's great when people surprise you.

Meeting Paul McCartney was a very obvious highlight, and of course, the other person who blew my mind was Tina Turner. She will always have a huge place in my heart.

I met some great people when I got invited to the Grand National in 2013, but I embarrassed my poor husband terribly.

A friend of ours, Judy Halewood, sponsored that year's Grand National, and she had invited a group of her friends along. When we sat down for lunch, I found myself next to Sir Alex Ferguson. Me, of all people. I know nothing about football; I'm much more into rugby. I know people say that Sir Alex can be a bit of a miserable sod, and he was quiet at first, but I soon had him laughing, and he was great. So many people were coming up and asking for pictures with him that, in the end, I told him I needed one too.

I can talk to anybody, really, and in this business, you get invited to so many events and meet lots of different people. I always like to introduce myself. Some people don't bother, and I find that strange. There was a chap sitting right opposite me, and I said to him, 'Hi, I'm Bonnie. Who are you?' It turned out it was Geoff Hurst, who scored the winning goal in the 1966 World Cup. He was so lovely, but Robert was sitting next to me, dying of shame.

I suppose you can't get bigger than meeting the Pope, either. I'm not Catholic, but it was still an honour to meet him when I was invited to perform at the Vatican Christmas Concert in 2019, alongside Susan Boyle and Lionel Ritchie. You don't stop and chat with him or anything; he just shakes your hand and you move on. But it was quite something, and I treasure the photo we have with him. It was a great honour. The party after the show was amazing. The food was incredible, and everything was so opulent. It's up there as one of my greatest career moments. The things I've had the opportunity to do as a result of singing are so special.

People probably assume that I'm hanging out with stars all the time, but that's not true at all. I'm so busy working that anytime I'm not, I like to relax by the pool if we're in Portugal or just listen to music back home in Wales. I'm certainly not having lavish dinner parties with A-listers. I'm much happier working on my music or enjoying time well spent with my family.

*

I'm really excited to be back in the studio working on a new album with David Mackay, but I'm going to be taking more control with this one because David and I are going to be doing everything ourselves. We'll work on the album collaboratively, and David will produce it. David will work his magic, and I'll sing my heart out, and we'll release a few tracks at a time online.

I've already done some vocals, but the album is on the back burner for the moment because my old record company have decided they're going to release a live album I recorded in Berlin. I don't mind, because it gives me and David a bit more time. I want to make these tracks very special.

I know I'm in my early seventies now, but I've got no plans to retire. I've never had a retirement plan. I've still got loads of gigs coming up, and I'm always being booked in for more, so I can't complain. Why stop doing what you love just because you're getting older? As long as I can get up on stage and belt out my hits, I will. I feel like a teenager when I'm performing. I have nothing to prove, but I do it because I love it.

And I still have plenty of energy. I've always had a lot, and I reckon I get it from my parents. My mother was always running around looking after us kids, and my father was always buzzing around doing things. Once he'd recovered from the tuberculosis, he lived a very full life. He was always on the go and certainly wasn't one to sit around doing nothing.

I remember asking my mother what it was like to reach seventy. She replied, 'You're only as young as you feel. I feel like I'm in my thirties.'

I feel the same. I still feel young, even though I know I'm not, and I've done so much in my life.

I was never fiercely ambitious. I always dreamed of singing when I watched *Top of the Pops* all those years ago, but I didn't have that steely determination so many people think you need to have if you're going to 'make it'. You hear stories about singers who are so desperate to succeed that they'll try for years and years, and they'll step over people to get to the top. That was never going to be me. As I've mentioned, after my first few hits, I would have been very happy to move back home and live a normal life singing in the clubs again. The fame and the showbiz life don't mean much to me. I just love to sing.

Even when things haven't been going as well as they could have, I have somehow managed to focus on the good things. I've coped with the rollercoaster of fame because I haven't changed, and I've never craved attention. I also wonder if staying positive and knowing that good things could be just around the corner has helped me to keep going and get up time and time again. I think attitude is everything in life. I also think having a solid family and a good friendship group around you makes a huge difference.

I've been so lucky that I've got to meet incredible people

and travel to places I never thought I'd have the chance to go to. But none of it made sense or made me feel fulfilled until Robert started travelling with me. That's when everything changed.

I've been incredibly lucky to have Robert by my side throughout everything.

We're still so in love now, and we have so many amazing memories to look back on and smile about – like the time we went for dinner at the Plaza Hotel in New York for our twenty-fifth wedding anniversary.

I decided I was going to make a real event of it, so I put on my original veil and tiara, which I had snuck into my suitcase. I wore it down to the restaurant, and I didn't give a shit who was looking at me. And people *were* looking. But they were also coming over and congratulating Robert and me, and some people even bought us champagne to celebrate. I never say no to a glass of champagne!

My life would have been so, so different without Robert in it. To this day, I look at him and think how lucky I am that we've got to live such a fabulous life together.

I may not have had a lot when I was growing up, but I've had a very blessed life, and I don't take any of it for granted. I'm glad I've got some good stories to tell, but I think everyone has good stories. Your life is just as interesting as mine, maybe just in a different way. I cannot say this often enough – no one is better than anyone else in this world. Some people are born into royalty, and some people are born into poverty, but no matter how much wealth or fame or privilege you have, everyone will have good times, and everyone will have challenges. You can't wish for anything better than good health, and as long as I'm healthy, I'm going to make the most of my life.

*

These last five years working with David Mackay – as well as many wonderful people that have been there for most of my career – have been indescribable. I am having the most fun.

I feel very lucky, and I count my blessings and cherish every moment. I grew up with a wonderful family, I've had a fantastic career I still enjoy to this day, and I've had my incredible husband by my side every step of the way. What more could I have asked for? Although I will say that not everything was handed to me on a plate. I may have got an initial break, but I've worked extremely hard since.

If I had one dream for the future, it would be to play Wembley Stadium. That's something that's always been in the back of my mind. If it doesn't happen, that's fine too. I have always believed in fate and that what's meant for you will come to you; your path is set out for you, no matter how many wishes you make. I truly believe Roger Bell was supposed to go to the wrong floor of the Townsman Club that night and send my life in an amazing, unexpected direction.

I may have done some extraordinary things over the past fifty years, but in so many ways I'm still that young girl from Wales, dancing around the piano with her family – and I always will be.

I like to think I've made the most of every day of my life, and I will continue to do so. And who knows?

Maybe the best really is yet to come.

Acknowledgements

First and foremost, thank you to my wonderful husband Robert for everything. I simply couldn't have done any of this without you by my side. And I'm so grateful for the love and support of my family over the years. Many of them are mentioned in the book already, but I'd like to give a personal round of thanks to them here.

Lots of love and thanks to my eldest sister Marlene, her husband Gwyn and their two wonderful children; to Margaret, my handsome brother Lynn's widow, and their four children; to my sister Angela, her three children and her wife Jan; to my sister Avis, whose lovely husband Billy is sadly no longer with us, and the three children they had together; and last but not least, to our little brother Paul, his wife Teresa and their two children.

Robert comes from a smaller but just as loving family, and I'd also like to thank them for the love, support and friendship over the years. So, thank you, Michael (that's Robert's brother), his wife Winnie and their two children; and Robert's stepbrother Paul, his wife Angie and their two children.

Lots of love and thanks to my brilliant nephews and nieces (all sixteen of them!), who amaze me with everything they do. And at the time of writing, I'm so blessed to have another fourteen great-nephews and great-nieces, who all bring me so much joy and happiness.

Matt Davis, Roger Bell, David Mackay (who I'm still working with to this day) and my digital wizards Liam and David – thanks for keeping the show on the road! Thanks also to all the amazing songwriters and producers I've worked with during my career, and to my awesome band: Ed Poole, Matt Prior, John Young and Alex Toff.

Huge thanks to Jordan Paramor for helping me to tell my story, and also to Hannah Black, Tom Atkins, Janet Aspey, Maria Garbutt-Lucero, Joelle Owusu-Sekyere and Matt Everett at Coronet for making this book happen.

And finally, to everyone who's reading this and listening to me after all this time – thank you, and God bless.

Picture Credits

All photos © author's personal collection, except:

p. 4, bottom right: © Terry Lott/Sony Music Archive via Getty Images.

p. 6, top: © David Redfern/Getty Images.

p. 7, top right: © Servizio Fotografico Vaticano.

p. 8, bottom left: © Ragnar Singsaas/Getty Images; bottom right: © PA Images/Alamy Stock Photo.